Puchta · Stranks · Lewis-Jones

MORE! 2
GRAMMAR PRACTICE

HELBLING

Mit Bescheid vom 2. Dezember 2009, GZ: BMUKK-5.001/0029-V/9/2009, hat das Bundesministerium für Unterricht, Kunst und Kultur das Unterrichtsmittel „MORE! Grammar Practice 2" von Puchta u.a. antragsgemäß in der vorliegenden Fassung gemäß §14 Abs. 2 und 5 des Schulunterrichtsgesetzes, BGBl. Nr. 472/86 und gemäß den derzeit geltenden Lehrplänen als für den Unterrichtsgebrauch an Hauptschulen und an allgemein bildenden höheren Schulen für die Klasse 2 im Unterrichtsgegenstand Englisch (1. lebende Fremdsprache) zur Aufnahme in den Anhang zu den Schulbuchlisten empfohlen.

MORE! 2 GRAMMAR PRACTICE

by
Herbert Puchta
Jeff Stranks
Peter Lewis-Jones

www.helbling.com

Design and layout by Amanda Hockin

Illustrated by Roberto Battestini, Giovanni Giorgi Pierfranceschi, Lorenzo Sabbatini, Nicola Zanni

Printed by Athesia

First published 2010

Third edition 2018, Second print run 2019

ISBN 978-3-85272-224-5

Schulbuchnummer: 146.077

Acknowledgements
The publishers would like to thank the following for their kind permission to reproduce the following photographs and other copyright material:
Alamy p39 (Spain winning the World Cup in 2010); **Dreamstime** p38 (women); **Wikimedia Commons** p39 (Spain winning the World Cup in 2010); **©iStockphoto.com** p20; **NASA/Bill Ingalls** p39 (Queen Elisabeth II); **Shutterstock** p38, p39, p54, 57.

Contents

Introduction

Liebe Schülerin!
Lieber Schüler!

Wenn du Sport betreibst, ist es für dich selbstverständlich, dass du regelmäßig trainierst. Wer im Schwimmen, beim Laufen, im Fußball oder beim Tischtennis seine Leistung verbessern will, merkt bald, dass regelmäßiges Üben zu besseren Resultaten führt. Aber nicht nur das – wer mehrfach wöchentlich trainiert, hat auch mehr Spaß am Üben, und was zuerst vielleicht etwas mühsam erscheint, gelingt bald viel besser und fast mühelos.

Mit dem Grammatiküben ist das nicht anders. Wer regelmäßig übt, macht bald weniger Fehler, erzielt bessere Ergebnisse und hat außerdem mehr Spaß an der Sprache. Die Übungen in diesem Buch und auf der beiliegenden e·ZONE sind so gebaut, dass sie garantiert bessere Lernleistungen bringen, wenn du sie regelmäßig durchführst. Also, am besten nicht etwa kurz vor einem Test ein paar Stunden üben! Du wirst bessere Resultate erzielen, wenn du dich mehrfach wöchentlich mit Grammatik beschäftigst. Dann brauchst du auch nicht so lange zu üben. Wie wär's mit 10 Minuten vier mal pro Woche? Versuch's mal – die ersten positiven Resultate werden sich einstellen!

Im Buch und auf der e·ZONE findest du die folgenden Hilfen:

- Das Inhaltsverzeichnis – zum schnellen Auffinden des Grammatikkapitels, das du üben möchtest.
- Jedes Grammatikkapitel beginnt mit einer Zusammenfassung der wichtigsten Formen und Regeln.
- Neben der Zusammenfassung findest du meist eine Ankündigung von Professor Grammar. Wenn du dieses Symbol siehst, solltest du am besten gleich mal in die e·ZONE schauen.
- Professor Grammar wird dir auf der e·ZONE im Abschnitt *How it works* helfen, eine Struktur besser zu verstehen. Im Bereich *Check it out* kannst du dann gleich mal versuchen, ob du die Erklärungen richtig verstanden hast.
- Nun kannst du wählen, ob du mit Hilfe der e·ZONE weiterüben möchtest, oder zuerst mit dem Buch arbeitest. Auf der e·ZONE findest du zu jedem Grammatikkapitel zwei oder drei Übungen, zum Beispiel Sätze mit Lücken, in die du die richtige Form einsetzen musst. Du kannst hier wählen, ob du dir zuerst die richtigen Lösungen anhören möchtest (*Listen*), und dann die Übung machen willst, oder ob du zuerst die Übung versuchen willst um sie dir vielleicht anschließend anzuhören.
- Im Buch selbst findest du zu jedem Grammatikkapitel eine oder mehrere Seiten an Übungen. Sie sind so angeordnet, dass du zuerst leichtere Übungen vorfindest und der Schwierigkeitsgrad allmählich gesteigert wird.
- Im Anhang zum Buch findest du eine Zusammenstellung aller Grammatikkapitel, die im Buch behandelt werden, mit Schautafeln, die dir eine gute Übersicht geben und den wichtigsten Regeln. Falls du mal ein Wort nicht kennen solltest, kannst du es in der Wordlist im Anhang nachschlagen. Außerdem findest du im Anhang auch die Lösungen – die solltest du dir am besten immer dann anschauen, wenn du deine Leistungen überprüfen möchtest, oder dich bei einem Kapitel mal gar nicht auskennst. Was wenig Sinn macht ist das regelmäßige Ansehen der Lösungen, bevor du eine Übung machst. Aber das weißt du ja selbst und auch hier gilt, was im Training im Sport gilt: Wer schummelt, beschummelt sich selbst.
- Und nun noch ein Tipp zum Schluss: auf der e·ZONE findest du zu jedem Grammatikkapitel einen *Cartoon* mit einem lustigen Rätsel.
- Ja, und dann hat Professor Grammar sich auch gelegentlich Tricks ausgedacht, um dir besonderen Lernspaß zu bereiten! Aber nun geht's los.

Viel Spaß und viel Erfolg wünschen dir die Autoren!

Herbert Puchta
Jeff Stranks
Peter Lewis-Jones

Present simple

Hello! See me on the e-ZONE to discover more about *present simple* and to learn better when to use it.

Das *present simple* verwendest du, wenn du beschreiben möchtest, was jemand immer wieder tut, was immer wieder geschieht oder was jemand fühlt. In Fragen und verneinten Sätzen fügst du **do/does** bzw. **don't/doesn't** hinzu.

Where **do** you live?	I live in Birmingham.	I **don't** live in London.
Where **does** she live?	She lives in Manchester.	She **doesn't** live in Leeds.

1 Write the 3rd person form of the verbs.

1 I like – He likes
2 I watch – He ....
3 I play – He ....
4 I am – He ....
5 I eat – He ....
6 I go – He ....
7 I talk – He ....
8 I wash – He ....
9 I leave – He ....
10 I buy – He ....
11 I switch – He ....
12 I have – He ....

2 Complete the sentences with the negative form of the verb and a word from the box.

football
novels
French
ham
~~red~~
the news
hip-hop
her sister

1 I wear black but I don't wear red .
2 Jack watches sports shows but he ....
3 Linda plays volleyball but she ....
4 Ian and Sophie study German but they ....
5 My parents listen to rock but they ....
6 You eat bacon but you ....
7 I like Mary but I ....
8 Trevor reads magazines but he ....

3 Rewrite the sentences and make them negative.

1 I like spaghetti.
I don't like spaghetti.

2 He lives in London.
....

3 You know Peter.
....

4 They play volleyball every Sunday.
....

5 Liam likes Jessica.
....

6 She wants to be a pilot.
....

7 Jenny and Rob are teachers.
....

8 We run 5 km every day.
....

e·ZONE **4** **Complete the text with the present simple form of the verbs.**

Hi, my name [1] ....*is*.......... (be) Oliver and my best friend [2] .... (be) Paul. My best friend and I [3] .... (be) completely different. For example, he [4] .... (like) Geography and History, I [5] .... (like) Art and Music. He [6] .... (want) to be an archaeologist when he [7] .... (leave) school. I [8] .... (want) to be a film director. He really [9] .... (enjoy) all sports. I [10] .... (not like) sport at all. I [11] .... (spend) all of my money on music. Guess what? He [12] .... (not listen) to music. He always [13] .... (wear) black. I [14] .... (not like) black. My favourite colour [15] .... (be) blue. He [16] .... (hate) blue of course. I think there [17] .... (be) only two things we have in common*: our age – we [18] .... (be) both 14 – and we both [19] .... (like) the same girl, Betty Hands. Betty [20] .... (be) his girlfriend but I [21] .... (like) her too. Paul [22] .... (not know) this. I [23] .... (not be) sure we are going to be best friends for much longer.

*__in common__ – etwas gemeinsam haben

5 **Use the text to write the questions for the answers.**

1 *What's Oliver's best friend called*?
He's called Paul.

2 ....?
His favourite subjects are Geography and History.

3 ....?
He wants to be a film director.

4 ....?
No, he doesn't. He hates sport.

5 ....?
He buys a lot of music.

6 ....?
Blue.

7 ....?
They are both 14.

8 ....?
No, he doesn't know anything.

6 **Write answers to the questions for you and your best friend.**

	me
1 How old are you?	*I'm* ....
2 What are your favourite school subjects?	....
3 What kind of clothes do you usually wear?	....
4 What sports do you enjoy doing?	....
5 What do you usually spend your money on?	....
6 What job do you want to do when you're older?	....
7 What music do you listen to?	....
8 What do you usually do on a Saturday?	....

7 **Write a short text about you and your friend. Use the information in 6 to help you.**

My best friend is called .... We're both .... His favourite school subject is .... but my favourite is ....

....

8 **Use the pictures to complete the table.**

On Mondays I		......play tennis......		but I don't go swimming.
On Tuesdays I		....		....
On Wednesdays I		....		....
On Thursdays I		....		....
On Fridays I		....		....
On Saturdays I		....		....
On Sundays I		....		....

And now go to the e-ZONE and do the Cartoon for Fun!

Past simple – revision

Hello! See me on the e·ZONE to discover more about *past simple – revision* and to learn better when to use it.

Wenn du etwas erzählst, was in der Vergangenheit passierte, verwendest du das *past simple*. Es gibt regelmäßige und unregelmäßige Formen.

I lik**ed** the present.	We **went** to the beach yesterday.

1 Find ten verbs and write them under the pictures.

E	A	T	L	A	H	K	D
P	W	E	L	C	N	R	L
B	R	E	A	K	W	S	O
M	Q	M	F	U	T	I	H
K	O	S	T	J	Y	T	M
D	N	I	F	P	E	O	L
L	U	V	G	H	C	B	Y
F	R	D	R	E	V	I	G

eat — ate

.... — ....

.... — ....

.... — ....

.... — ....

.... — ....

.... — ....

.... — ....

.... — ....

.... — ....

2 Tick the sentences that have got an irregular past tense in them.

1 She ran down the road and fell over. ☑

2 She phoned me and invited me to her party. ☐

3 We walked on the beach and played volleyball. ☐

4 He looked out of the window and saw me. ☐

5 She held his hand and kissed him. ☐

6 He climbed up the tree and jumped down again. ☐

7 We played tennis and then we went home. ☐

8 He read his book for five minutes and then he turned out the lights. ☐

3 Use the past form of the verbs to complete the sentences.

Everyone ....had.......... (have) great summer holidays.
Victor [1].................................. (play) volleyball on a French beach.
Harry [2].................................. (hold) hands with a Spanish girl on a Spanish beach.
Diana [3].................................. (drive) with her dad in a BMW down a German motorway.
Eddie [4].................................. (eat) ice cream in Venice.
Simon [5].................................. (swim) in the warm ocean in South Africa.
Jimmy [6].................................. (go) trekking in the wild Brazilian jungles.
Maggie [7].................................. (meet) famous film stars in LA.
Kelly [8].................................. (kiss) a handsome Italian in Rome.
Phil [9].................................. (fly) first class to Australia.
And me? I [10].................................. (have) a lovely time here at home reading all their postcards.

e·ZONE

4 Complete the text with the past forms of the verbs in the box.

eat
give
~~wake up~~
go
dream
watch
meet
walk

1 Yesterday was perfect. I ......woke up...... late.
2 I .... bacon and eggs for breakfast.
3 I .... DVDs all morning.
4 After lunch I .... roller-skating with my friends in the park.
5 I also .... Kevin Maley in the park.
6 He .... me a rose.
7 Then he .... home with me.
8 I .... about Kevin all night. I can't wait until tomorrow!

5 Write about your 'perfect yesterday'.

....

....

....

....

And now go to the e·ZONE and do the Cartoon for Fun!

Past simple – negation

Wenn du mit der *past simple* Form eines Verbs etwas verneinen möchtest, verwendest du **didn't (=did not)** zusammen mit der Grundform des Verbs.

+	–
(work) I/You/He/She/It/We/They **worked**.	I/You/He/She/It/We/They **didn't work**.
(go) I/You/He/She/It/We/They **went** to school.	I/You/He/She/It/We/They **didn't go**.
(be) I/He/She/It **was** there.	I/He/She/It **wasn't** there.
You/We/They **were** there.	You/We/They **weren't** there.

1 Match the pictures and sentences.

1 We didn't enjoy our holiday last year.
2 The weather wasn't nice at all.
3 We didn't like the hotel.
4 The food wasn't very good.
5 The room was noisy so we didn't sleep well.
6 My mother didn't like the shops.
7 Dad and I didn't see the football match.
8 The good thing was – we went home after three days!

e-ZONE 2 Write the phrases in the correct places.

asked
didn't ask
went
didn't go
saw
didn't see
~~worked~~
didn't work

1 My dad ...worked... very hard yesterday, so when he came home he was very tired.
2 I didn't know the answer to the questions, so I phoned my friend Gill and .... her to help me.
3 Last year we went to New York – and I .... lots of famous people!
4 We .... to the cinema last night – the film was great!
5 The question was very difficult, so I was happy that the teacher .... me to answer it!
6 I .... on Friday night or Saturday, so I had to do all my homework on Sunday night.
7 I was really ill on Friday, so I .... to school.
8 **A** Was John at school yesterday? **B** I'm not sure – I .... him.

And now go to the e-ZONE and do the Cartoon for Fun!

Past simple – questions

Hello! See me on the e·ZONE to discover more about *past simple – questions* and to learn better when to use them.

Wenn du mit der *past simple* Form eines Verbs eine Frage stellen möchtest, verwendest du **did** zusammen mit der Grundform des Verbs.

Statement	Question
(work) I/You/He/She/It/We/They **worked**.	**Did** I/you/he/she/it/we/they **work**?
(go) I/You/He/She/It/We/They **went** to school.	**Did** I/you/he/she/it/we/they **go** to school?
(be) I/He/She/It **was** there.	**Was** I/he/she/it there?
You/We/They **were** there.	**Were** you/we/they there?

1 Put the words in the correct order to make the questions. Then match them to the answers.

1 your / Was / good / holiday?
Was your holiday good?

2 brother and sister / your / with / go / Did / you?
....

3 hotel / you / in / Did / a / stay?
....

4 own / you / food / cook / your / Did?
....

☐ Sometimes – but we went to restaurants too.
[1] Yes, it was great, thanks!
☐ No, I went with some friends.
☐ No, we didn't. We went camping.

e·ZONE **2 Write the questions and the answers. Use the verbs in the box.**

go
~~see~~
watch
do

1 A ....Did.... you ....see.... Annie yesterday?
B No, I .... Annie – but I saw Julia.

2 A .... you .... the Maths homework last night?
B Yes, I did – but I .... the French homework.

3 A .... you .... to Italy on holiday?
B No, we .... to Italy – we went to Spain.

4 A .... you .... the football match last night?
B No, I .... football – I watched the science-fiction film.

3 Complete the questions. Then answer them for you.

1 you / go / town / yesterday?
Did you go to town yesterday?
Yes, I did. / No, I didn't.

2 you / see / friends / last Saturday?
....
....

3 the teacher / give you / homework / last night?
....
....

4 your parents / go out / last weekend?
....
....

And now go to the e·ZONE and do the Cartoon for Fun!

Past simple – negation and questions

1 Put the dialogue in the correct order.

- ☐ **A** Which friends? Jimmy Hardy?
- ☐ **A** You walked around the shopping centre?
- ☐ **A** The shopping centre? Did you buy anything?
- 1 **A** So where did you go last night?
- ☐ **A** I just want to know what to give you for breakfast!
- ☐ **A** No food? Hmm – so are you hungry this morning?
- ☐ **B** I went to the shopping centre.
- ☐ **B** No – I didn't meet Jimmy, I met Andy and Jack. We didn't do much – we just walked around.
- ☐ **B** Yes, because we didn't have any money. So we couldn't buy anything and we didn't eat any food.
- ☐ **B** Yes, I'm very hungry! But mum – why all these questions?
- ☐ **B** No, I didn't go shopping – I just met my friends.

2 Circle the correct options.

1 … out last Saturday night?
a You went **b** Did you go **c** Go you

2 … you in town yesterday?
a Was **b** Are **c** Were

3 We went to the cinema, but we … the film.
a not liked **b** did like not **c** didn't like

4 I phoned Johnny, but he … at home.
a wasn't **b** weren't **c** didn't be

e·ZONE 3 Complete the dialogue. Put the verbs into the correct form.

A Where [1] did you go (go) last night?
B To the cinema.
A Who [2] .... (go) with you?
B I went with Paula. I invited Ashley – but Ashley [3] .... (not come).
A Oh dear. Well – what [4] .... (be) the film like?
B The film [5] .... (not be) very good. I [6] .... (not like) it. But there was one good thing: I [7] .... (not pay).

A You didn't pay?
B No. I [8] .... (not have) any money. Paula paid.
A Oh. Where [9] .... (go) after the cinema?
B We went to a pizza place – but I [10] .... (not be) hungry, so I [11] .... (not eat) anything. Paula [12] .... (not have) anything, either.
A What [13] .... (talk) about?
B We [14] .... (not talk) about anything. I [15] .... (not want) to talk to Paula.
A It sounds like a wonderful evening.
B It [16] .... (not be) a wonderful evening. It was terrible!
A I know – I was joking!

And now go to the e·ZONE and do the Cartoon for Fun!

Irregular verbs

Regular	Irregular
play – play**ed**	go – **went**
talk – talk**ed**	read – **read**

H	B	R	O	K	E	S	N	T
A	R	G	E	T	W	E	N	T
F	O	G	O	T	O	C	A	G
O	K	R	P	O	G	A	V	A
U	E	E	E	O	L	U	E	V
N	D	A	A	K	P	G	R	E
D	C	D	R	E	A	H	E	V
W	O	H	A	D	E	T	D	E
E	N	T	H	A	S	A	I	D

1 Find the past forms. Write them beside the verbs.

1 go – went
2 break – ....
3 find – ....
4 give – ....
5 get – ....
6 have – ....
7 catch – ....
8 say – ....
9 read – ....
10 take – ....

2 Use the verbs from 1 to complete the sentences.

1 Yesterday I went into town.
2 I didn't watch TV last night – I .... a book!
3 My mother .... something to me, but I didn't hear her.
4 For Christmas last year, I .... a new bicycle from my parents.
5 I was dirty from playing football, so when I got home I .... a bath.
6 I was lucky yesterday – I .... a £20 note in the street.
7 My brother went fishing yesterday – he .... six fish!
8 We went on holiday to Greece last year – I .... hundreds of photos!
9 Last Friday, the teacher .... us lots of homework for the weekend.
10 Mary was angry with me because I .... her new MP3-player.

e·ZONE **3 Complete the story with the correct form of the verbs.**

Last Wednesday night, I [1] went (go) into town. My father [2]........................ (take) me in his car and he [3]........................ (say) he was coming to pick me up. I [4]........................ (go) to the cinema and I [5]........................ (watch) a film – it wasn't really very good. After the film, I [6]........................ (wait) for my dad outside the cinema. It [7]........................ (be) really cold!
Then my dad [8]........................ (phone) me. He said: 'Sorry, I can't come. Catch the bus! See you later.'

But I [9]........................ (not have) any money for the bus. So I [10]........................ (start) to walk home. But then it [11]........................ (start) to rain. I [12]........................ (get) very wet. So I [13]........................ (stop) in the door of a bank.
Then I [14]........................ (look) down at the floor – and I [15]........................ (find) some money! There [16]........................ (be) a two-pound coin on the ground. I [17]........................ (pick) it up and [18]........................ (run) to the bus stop. I [19]........................ (catch) the last bus home. Lucky me!

And now go to the e·ZONE and do the Cartoon for Fun!

one – ones

Hello! See me on the e-ZONE to discover more about *one – ones* and to learn better when to use them.

Wenn du ein Nomen nochmals erwähnen möchtest, das bereits im Satz davor vorkam, kannst du es durch **one** (singular) oder **ones** (plural) ersetzen.

I don't like the green **T-shirt**.	I like the blue **one**.
Do you want the pink or blue **jeans**?	The blue **ones**.

1 Match the questions and answers.

1 Which pizza would you like?
2 Which gym do you go to?
3 Which film do you want to see?
4 Which films do you like best?
5 Which T-shirt do you want?
6 Which jeans do you want?
7 Which girls are your sisters?
8 Which girl is your sister?

a The ones wearing red shoes.
b The one in the High Street opposite the bank.
c The blue ones.
d The blue one.
e The one with ham and mushrooms on it.
f The one wearing red shoes.
g Ones with Brad Pitt in them!
h The one with Brad Pitt in it.

2 Complete the dialogues with *one* or *ones*.

1 **A** Would you like a sandwich?
B Yes, please. .... with cheese
2 **A** Did you buy some jeans?
B Yes, I bought the blue ....
3 **A** Did you watch that horror film?
B No, we watched a detective ....
4 **A** Did the robber take all the paintings?
B No, just the .... in the library.
5 **A** Which boy hit you?
B That .... in the green T-shirt.
6 **A** Do you like these shoes?
B I like the green .... better.

e-ZONE 3 Underline the correct words. (A = Assistant, D = Dave.)

A Hello, can I help you?
D Yes, I'd like to try on some sunglasses – the [1]*one / ones* over there in the window.
A These [2]*one / ones*?
D No, the [3]*one / ones* next to the green cap.
A Which [4]*one / ones*? There are lots of green caps in the window.
D The [5]*one / ones* with red bits on it.
A This [6]*one / ones*?
D No! No, not that [7]*one / ones*, the red and green cap next to the sunglasses.
A This [8]*one / ones*?
D Yes.
A And you want to try this [9]*one / ones* on?
D No, I don't want to try a cap on. I want to try on the sunglasses. The [10]*one / ones* next to that cap.

A These [11]*one / ones*.
D Yes. Yes, those [12]*one / ones*.
A I'm sorry. These sunglasses aren't for sale.

And now go to the e-ZONE and do the Cartoon for Fun!

why / because

Mit dem Fragewort **why?** fragst du nach einer Begründung („warum"). Mit **because** beantwortest du eine **why**-Frage.

e-ZONE **1 Match the jokes and the answers.**

1 *Why didn't the skeleton go to the party?*

2 *Why is 6 scared of 7?*

3 *Why is V a monster?*

4 *Why was the computer cold?*

5 *Why do birds sit on their eggs?*

6 *Why did the Maths book cry?*

7 *Why do you go to bed every night?*

8 *Why did the elephant wear red shoes?*

9 *Why do birds fly south in the winter?*

a Because it always comes after U. ◯

b Because it didn't close its windows. ◯

c Because it's too far to walk. ◯

d Because the bed doesn't come to you. ◯

e Because they don't have chairs. ◯

f Because his white ones were dirty. ◯

g Because 7 ate 9. ◯

h Because he had no body to go with. ◯

i Because it had so many problems. ◯

2 Complete the dialogues with *why* or *because*.

1 A ....Why.... was she angry?
B .... our dog bit her.

2 A I didn't go to the party.
B .... not?
A .... I was really tired.

3 A We don't like our teacher .... he gives us a lot of homework.
B .... does he do that?
A .... he thinks we have to work harder.

4 A .... are you crying?
B .... nobody remembered my birthday.

5 A We're lost.
B .... didn't you bring a map?
A .... I haven't got one.

6 A I didn't phone you .... I haven't got your number.
B .... haven't you got my number?
A .... you never gave it to me.

3 Read the text. Then complete the questions.

On Friday night, Jamie went to bed late. He was very tired and he forgot to put his alarm clock on. On Saturday morning, he didn't wake up until 10 o'clock. Jamie looked at the clock. 10 o'clock! The football match started at 10.30 – he was late! He jumped out of bed and got dressed as quickly as possible. He ran downstairs. The house was empty – his mum and dad were at the shops. He opened the fridge – empty, too. So, no breakfast. No problem, he wasn't very hungry. Jamie got on his bike and cycled as fast as he could to the place where the football match was going to start. He got there at 10.25. The teacher looked surprised when he saw Jamie – Jamie's face was all red. 'OK, Jamie,' he said. 'You're just in time. Go and put your football things on.' 'Oh no!' shouted Jamie. His football kit was in his bag – back at home, in his bedroom!

1 Why didn't Jamie wake up until 10 o'clock?
Because he forgot to put his alarm clock on.

2 ....
.... out of bed?
Because he was late.

3 ....
.... empty?
Because his parents were at the shops.

4 ....
.... breakfast?
Because there was no food in the fridge.

5 ....
.... surprised?
Because Jamie's face was all red.

6 ....
.... 'Oh no!'?
Because his football things were back at home.

4 Use your imagination. Write the missing answers and questions.

1 A Why didn't you eat your sandwich?
B Because I wasn't hungry.

2 A ....?
B Because I didn't have any money.

3 A Why didn't you play football this afternoon?
B ....

4 A ....?
B Because I don't like pets.

5 A Why do you always wear black?
B ....

6 A ....?
B Because it was too scary.

And now go to the e-ZONE and do the Cartoon for Fun!

should / shouldn't

Hello! See me on the e-ZONE to discover more about *should / shouldn't* and to learn better when to use them.

Wenn du sagen möchtest, was jemand tun oder nicht tun soll, verwendest du nach der Person **should** oder **shouldn't (=should not)** zusammen mit der Grundform des Verbs.

You **should do** some exercise.	You **shouldn't eat** so quickly.
We **should go** home now.	They **shouldn't make** so much noise.

1 Match the pictures and sentences.

1 It's late. We should go home now.
2 You shouldn't eat so quickly.
3 They shouldn't make so much noise.
4 He should be careful.
5 Perhaps you should wash him.
6 You shouldn't look at my work.
7 We should call the police.
8 It's great – you should go and see it.
9 She shouldn't go to school for a few days.

2 Complete the dialogues. Use *should* or *shouldn't* and a phrase from the box.

charge it more often
go later
eat an apple
stay out late
go to bed early
call him bad names
worry so much
have a party

1 **A** I'm feeling really hungry.
B Well, perhaps you should eat an apple or something.

2 **A** I've got an important test tomorrow.
B Really? Well then, you should go to bed early and get some good sleep.

3 **A** I think Paul's angry with me.
B Of course he is! You really shouldn't call him bad names you know.

4 **A** I heard a noise! Perhaps it's a ghost.
B Don't be silly. You shouldn't worry so much .

5 **A** I'm sorry I didn't phone you. The battery in my mobile was flat.
B You always say that! You know, I think you should charge it more often .

6 **A** I'm going to be fifteen on Saturday.
B Great! We should have a party How about Sunday at my place?

7 **A** I want to go to the park and play football.
B Well, it's raining, so I think you should go later .

8 **A** I was really tired on Monday morning.
B It's not surprising. You shouldn't stay out late on Sunday nights!

e·ZONE **3** **Put the words in the correct order to make the sentences.**

1 home / You / at night / alone / shouldn't / walk
You shouldn't walk home alone at night.

2 sorry / you're / You / say / should
You should say you're sorry.

3 any / shouldn't / make / We / noise
We shouldn't make any noise.

4 dog / take / We / for a walk / should / this afternoon / the
We should take the dog for a walk this afternoon.

5 shouldn't / so / I / eat / chocolate / much
I shouldn't eat so much chocolate.

6 invite / cinema / We / should / the / to / him
We should invite him to the cinema.

4 **Which sentence from 3 goes with each picture? Write numbers.**

a

b

c

d

e

f

5 **Complete the sentences with *should / shouldn't* and your own ideas.**

I think that in school, we shouldn't run.

My friend is very tired. Perhaps he/she should go to bed.

I think my parents shouldn't go for a walk.

I want to be successful when I'm older. Perhaps I should have a ...

The authorities* in our town should give us a park.

***authorities** – Behörden

And now go to the e·ZONE and do the Cartoon for Fun!

Comparatives

Alle einsilbigen und einige zweisilbige Adjektive werden mit **-er** (Komparativ) und **-est** (Superlativ) gesteigert. Alle anderen Adjektive mit zwei Silben und alle drei- und viersilbigen steigerst du mit **more** und **most**.

Wie im Deutschen verwendest du für Vergleiche die Komparativform des Adjektivs. Achte auf die Schreibweise bei Adjektiven, an die du **-er** anhängst: **y** am Wortende wird zu **i**, **g** wird verdoppelt.

I'm old**er than** my brother.

I'm big**ger than** my sister.

I'm heav**ier than** my mum.

I'm **more** intelligent **than** my dad.

1 **Read the sentences and tick what's true.**

1 My pencil is longer than your pencil.

2 My school bag is heavier than your school bag.

3 Your dog is more intelligent than my dog.

4 My pet is more exotic than your pet.

5 My cat is prettier than your cat.

6 Your game console is more popular than my game console.

7 My bike is faster than your bike.

8 Your watch is more expensive than my watch.

2 Underline the correct words.

1 This table is really *heavy* / *heavier*. Can you help me?
2 I'm three days *old* / *older* than you.
3 The film is *good* / *better* than the book.
4 That snake looks *dangerous* / *more dangerous* than the other one.
5 The waves are always small here. It's a very *safe* / *safer* beach.
6 It was *cold* / *colder* yesterday than it is today.
7 Oliver is really *intelligent* / *more intelligent*. He always gets the best marks.
8 I was a very *ugly* / *uglier* baby, but look at me now!

e·ZONE 3 Complete the sentences using the same adjective.

1 Cape Town is beautiful but Rio de Janeiro is ....more beautiful.... .
2 Cheetahs are fast but antelopes are ....faster.... .
3 Kate Pimm is popular but Debbie Helps is ....more popular.... .
4 Porsches are expensive but Ferraris are ....more expensive.... .
5 Chimpanzees are intelligent but dolphins are ....more intelligent.... .
6 My first girlfriend was pretty but my new girlfriend is ....prettier.... .
7 Your problem is big but my problem is ....bigger.... .
8 That spider is poisonous but this one is ....more poisonous.... .

e·ZONE 4 Complete the poem with the comparative form of the adjectives.

My perfect cousin (a love poem)

I'm 1 ....older.... (old) than him but he's 2 ....taller.... (tall) than me.
(I'm one metre forty, he's one forty-three.)

I hate to say it but he's 3 ....more intelligent.... (intelligent) than me.
His last grade was A and my grade was C!

The girls all say he's 4 ....more handsome.... (handsome) than me.
(But I think he looks like an old chimpanzee!)

I think he must be 5 ....friendlier.... (friendly) than me.
He's got hundreds of friends. I've only got three!

He's got lots of money. He's 6 ....richer.... (rich) than me.
He's got an amazing new bike and a brand new TV.

He loves all sports and he's 7 ....better.... (good) than me.
He's 8 ....stronger.... (strong) and 9 ....faster.... (fast) and eats salad for tea!

Yes, he's got everything and he's great, my cousin Jim.
But with you by my side, I'm 10 ....happier.... (happy) than him.

And now go to the e·ZONE and do the Cartoon for Fun!

as ... as

So kannst du Gleichheit oder Ungleichheit beschreiben.

I'm **as** tall **as** you = We're the same height.

I'm **not as** tall **as** you. = You're taller than me.

1 Read the information card and write T (*True*) or F (*False*) for the sentences.

	T Rex	Stegosaurus	Triceratops
Height	5.6 m	3 m	3 m
Weight	6000 kg	3100 kg	5500 kg
Danger rating*	9	2	2
Intelligence rating	8	1	8

1 The Stegosaurus was not as dangerous as the T Rex. T
2 The Triceratops was as tall as the Stegosaurus. T
3 The T Rex was as intelligent as the Stegosaurus. T
4 The Triceratops was not as heavy as the T Rex. T
5 The T Rex was not as dangerous as the Stegosaurus. F
6 The Stegosaurus was not as tall as the T Rex. T
7 The Stegosaurus was as heavy as the T Rex. F
8 The Stegosaurus was not as dangerous as the Triceratops. F

*rating – Quote

2 Using the information in 1 write *(not)* *as ... as* sentences to compare:

1 Stegosaurus / T Rex (height) The Stegosaurus was not as tall as the T Rex.
2 Triceratops / T Rex (intelligence) The Triceratops was as intelligent as the T Rex
3 Triceratops / Stegosaurus (height) The Triceratops was as tall as the Stegosaurus
4 Triceratops / T Rex (danger) The Triceratops was not as dangerous as the T Rex

e-ZONE 3 Rewrite the sentences using *(not) as ... as*.

1 I'm taller than my mum. My mum's not as tall as me.
2 The film is funnier than the book. The film is not as funny as the book.
3 Mr Brown is more popular than Mr Thomas. Mr Thomas is not as popular as Mr Brown
4 Maths is more difficult than English. English is not as difficult as Maths.
5 Your present was more expensive than my present. My present was not as expensive as your present.
6 Football is more exciting than tennis. Tennis is not as exciting as football.

And now go to the e-ZONE and do the Cartoon for Fun!

Superlatives

Wenn du das höchste Maß von etwas beschreiben möchtest, verwendest du die Superlativform des Adjektivs. Du fügst auch **the** hinzu. Auch hier musst auf die Schreibweise achten: **y** am Wortende wird zu **i**, **g** wird verdoppelt.

I'm **the** old**est** in the class.
It's **the** big**gest** animal in the world.
She's **the** pretti**est** girl in the school.
He's **the most** intelligent person I know.

1 Complete the table.

adjective	comparative	superlative
old	older than	the oldest
new	newer than	the newest
tall	taller than	the tallest
hot	hotter than	the hottest
big	bigger than	the biggest
pretty	prettier than	the prettiest
heavy	heavier than	the heaviest
important	more important than	the most important
boring	more boring than	the most boring
relaxing	more relexing than	the most relaxing
good	better than	the best
bad	worse than	the worst

e-ZONE **2 Use phrases from 1 to complete the sentences.**

It was Sunday and it was 42°C. It was 1 the hottest day of the year! My school books were on the table in front of me. I had my final tests next week – 2 the most important tests of the year! Fail* and spend your summer holiday studying. I wanted to go to the beach. I looked at my books. 'Why is studying so boring? It's even 3 More boring than doing housework.' I thought. The phone rang. It was Diana Nicholls. Beautiful Diana Nicholls – 4 the prettiest girl in the school! What did she want with me? She wanted me to go to the beach. 'But the tests …?' I asked her.

'The tests!' she said. 'You need to relax. A day on the beach is 5 the most relaxing studying.' It was a good idea. In fact it was 6 the best idea of the day. 'OK.' I said.

I had a great time on the beach. It was definitely 7 better than studying at home.

And the tests? My grades were bad. Really bad. They were 8 the worst in the school.

Tomorrow is the first day of the summer holiday. Three weeks of studying for me. But that's no problem. The weather is cold (only 23°C) and my new girlfriend is going to study with me – Diana. Her grades were terrible too.

***fail** – durchfallen

3 Read about the four spies and put the symbols in the correct spaces in the table.

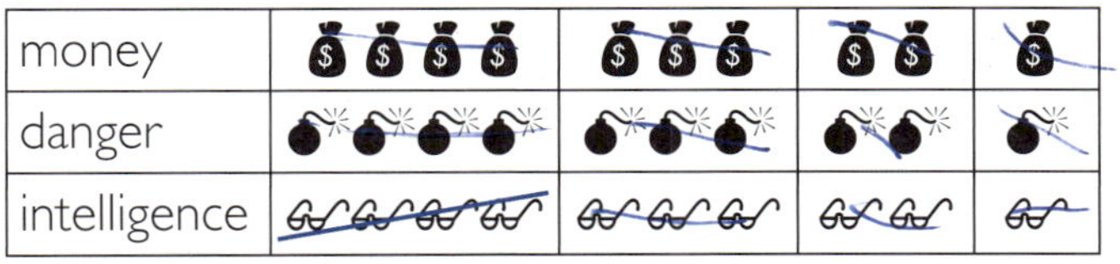

	Dick Spyder	Raymond Black	Edgar Peril	Lucy Diamond
money				
danger				
intelligence				

1 Edgar Peril is more intelligent than Raymond Black but he isn't as intelligent as Dick Spyder.
2 Lucy Diamond is richer than Edgar Peril.
3 Raymond Black is the second most dangerous.
4 Dick Spyder isn't as rich as Edgar Peril.
5 Edgar Peril is more dangerous than Raymond Black.
6 Lucy Diamond is the most intelligent.
7 Raymond Black is the richest.
8 Lucy Diamond isn't as dangerous as Dick Spyder.

4 Look at the completed table in 3 and complete the sentences.

1 Dick Spyder ...isn't as rich as... Edgar Peril. (rich)
2 Lucy Diamond ...isn't as intelligent as... Dick Spyder. (intelligent)
3 Raymond Black ...isn't as dangerous as... Edgar Peril. (dangerous)
4 Dick Spyder ...is more intelligent... Raymond Black. (intelligent)
5 Lucy Diamond ...is richer than... Dick Spyder. (rich)
6 Raymond Black ...isn't as intelligent as... Lucy Diamond. (intelligent)
7 Edgar Peril ...is the most dangerous... (dangerous)
8 Raymond Black ...is the richest... (rich)

5 Put the words in order.

Eight things you never knew about my family:

1 mum / than / taller / my / I'm
(but don't tell her)
I'm taller than my mum.

2 funniest / the / in / person / family / my / I'm
I'm the funniest person in my family.

3 pretty / as / I'm / my / mum / as
I'm as pretty as my mum.

4 older / than / dog / is / me / our
(by two weeks!)
Our dog is older than me.

5 as / my / intelligent / me / sister / isn't / as
(but she thinks she is)
My sister isn't as intelligent as me.

6 brother / my / is / me / youngest / than / older (it's possible – think about it)
My youngest brother is older than me.

7 thinks / isn't / funny / is / as / as / my / dad / he / he
My dad thinks he isn't as funny as he is.

8 but / richest / meanest* / dad / is / the / my / he's / also / the
My dad is the richest but he's also the meanest.

*mean – geizig

6 Write six similar facts about your family.

And now go to the e·ZONE and do the Cartoon for Fun!

Directions (prepositions of place)

e·ZONE **1 Write the words / phrases under the pictures.**

~~behind~~
~~in front of~~
~~next to~~
~~opposite~~
~~on the corner~~
~~round the corner~~

1

next to

2

in front of

3

round the corner

4

opposite

5

on the corner

6

behind

e·ZONE **2 Write the words in the correct order.**

1 the / on / it's / corner
It's on the corner.

2 corner / go / round / the
Go round the corner.

3 ahead / straight / go
Go straight ahead.

4 it's / front / bank / of / the / in
It's in front of the bank.

5 next / the / it's / to / supermarket
It's next to the supermarket.

6 take / right / the / first
Take the first right.

7 second / the / take / left
Take the second left.

3 Look at the map on page 25. Read the directions. Write the place you get to.

1 Go straight ahead. Take the first right. Go to the end of Queen Street. It's opposite the bank.
restaurant

2 Go straight ahead. Take the second left. Walk about 100 metres. It's next to the music shop.
post office

3 Go straight ahead. Take the third right. Go past the park. It's on your left.
church

4 Go straight ahead. Take the first left. Go to the end of the street. It's on the corner of West Street – opposite the chemist's.
cinema

5 Go straight ahead. Take the third left. It's at the end of the street – on the right, opposite the supermarket.
bank

6 Go straight ahead. Take the second right. Go past the post office. Turn left. It's on your right.
hospital

4 **Write directions for someone to get to the following places. Start from the bottom of High Street – the same as in 3.**

1 The restaurant in King Street: ....

....

2 The railway station: ....

....

3 The tourist office: ....

....

4 The café in Abbey Street: ....

....

5 The post office in North Street: ....

....

6 The bus station: ....

....

And now go to the e-ZONE and do the Cartoon for Fun!

have to / don't have to

Hello! See me on the e·ZONE to discover more about ***have to / don't have to*** and to learn better when to use them.

Wenn du sagen möchtest, dass jemand etwas tun muss, kannst du entweder **must** oder **have to/has to** zusammen mit der Grundform des Verbs verwenden. Wenn du aber sagen möchtest, dass jemand etwas nicht tun muss, oder nicht zu tun braucht, musst du **don't have to** oder **doesn't have to** verwenden, denn im Englischen bedeutet **mustn't** etwas ganz anderes, nämlich dass jemand etwas nicht darf.

I/You/We/They **have to go** now.	I/You/We/They **don't have to wear** a uniform.
He/She/It **has to be** good.	He/She/It **doesn't have to work**.

e·ZONE **1** **Match the sentences and the signs.**

a 

b 

c 

d 

e 

f 

1 You have to turn right here.
2 You don't have to pay to go in.
3 You have to be over 14.
4 You have to stop.
5 You have to pay to go in.
6 You don't have to know anything.

2 **Write the words in the correct order.**

1 up / I / to / get / have / on weekdays / early
I have to get up early on weekdays.
2 to / party / You / come / to / my / have
....
3 My / have / study / doesn't / hard / brother / to
....
4 for homework / has / She / write / to / a / story
....
5 have / go / tomorrow / We / don't / to / school / to
....
6 every weekend / my / have / to / I / tidy / room
....
7 do / don't / We / have / washing-up / to / the
....
8 you / wear / have / school / Do / a / to / uniform / to
....?

3 **Match the sentences to make mini-dialogues.**

1 Do you have to do homework every night?
2 Can you help me, please?
3 I don't want any breakfast, thanks.
4 Can I borrow your bike?
5 There's a free concert in the park.
6 Why can't I see this film?
7 I don't have to get up early tomorrow.
8 Your trainers are really old!

a OK – but you have to bring it back at 5.00.
b Why? Is it a holiday or something?
c No – I only have to do it on Fridays.
d Yes – I have to buy some new ones.
e Because you have to be over 14 to watch it.
f But you have to eat something before school!
g Sorry, no – I have to go out now.
h Great – so we don't have to pay!

e·ZONE **4** **Complete the text with the phrases in the box.**

Life at the Milky Way School for Martians

- don't have to be
- don't have to take
- don't have to switch
- don't have to work
- have to leave
- have to wave
- have to talk
- ~~have to wear~~
- have to use
- have to wiggle

At our school, we [1] ......*have to wear*...... a uniform – it's green and black and pink, our favourite colours! We go to school at 6 o'clock in the morning, and we [2] .... at 7 o'clock at night. We [3] .... our mobile phones off – in fact, we [4] .... our phones every 30 minutes, and we [5] .... very loudly, too. The school gives us 5 kilos of broccoli to eat in the break so we [6] .... our own food to school. When a teacher comes into the classroom, we [7] .... our arms around (all ten of them) and we [8] .... our ears (all six of them) – boring! Our favourite teacher is Mrs Gorgly – in her lessons, we [9] .... hard and we [10] .... quiet, either!

5 **Look at the table. Write sentences about the people.**

	Angus	Becky	Colin and Sally
wear a school uniform	✓	✗	✓
help with the housework	✗	✗	✓
study hard before a test	✓	✓	✗
leave home early to go to school	✗	✓	✗

1. Angus ...*has to wear a school uniform.*...
2. Angus ...*doesn't have to help with the housework.*...
3. Angus ....
4. Angus ....
5. Becky ....
6. Becky ....
7. Becky ....
8. Becky ....
9. Colin and Sally ....
10. Colin and Sally ....
11. Colin and Sally ....
12. Colin and Sally ....

6 **Now write sentences about YOU. Write about the activities in 5.**

I .... a school uniform.

I .... with the housework.

I ....

I ....

And now go to the e·ZONE and do the Cartoon for Fun!

going to – negative

Wenn du sagen möchtest, dass jemand plant oder vorhat, etwas nicht zu tun, verwendest du die verneinte Form von **be going to** mit der Grundform des Verbs.

I'**m not going to** help you.
You'**re not going to** like this.
He/She **isn't going to** watch TV all day.
It **isn't going to** rain tomorrow.
We'**re not going to** tell anybody.
They'**re not going to** play football this afternoon.

e·ZONE **1** **Complete the horoscope with the words in the box.**

going to meet	going to be	~~going to get~~	going to have
going to ask	going to fight	going to cook	going to give

Aries

April is going to be a fantastic month:

1 You're ....going to get.... the best grade in the test.
2 Your mum's .... your favourite dinner every day.
3 You're .... very popular with your class mates.
4 You're .... a new 'special' friend.
5 Your teacher isn't .... you any homework.
6 Your mum and dad aren't .... you to help in the house.
7 Your brothers and sisters aren't .... with you all day.
8 And you aren't .... any problems all month.

2 **Underline the correct options.**

Did you have a great April? Good – because May is going to be terrible!

1 *It's / It isn't* going to rain all month.
2 *You're / You aren't* going to fall off your bike – twice!
3 Your teacher *is / isn't* going to tell you off all the time.
4 Your dad *is / isn't* going to give you any pocket money.
5 Your brothers *are / aren't* going to break your computer.
6 Your friends *are / aren't* going to invite you to their party.
7 *You're / You aren't* going to be sad for 30 days.
8 Because *you're / you aren't* going to have any fun for a month.

And now go to the e·ZONE and do the Cartoon for Fun!

might (not)

Hello! See me on the e-ZONE to discover more about *might (not)* and to learn better when to use it.

Wenn du sagen möchtest, dass in Zukunft etwas vielleicht (nicht) sein könnte, oder jemand etwas (nicht) tun könnte, verwendest du **might** oder **might not** mit der Grundform des Verbs.

I/You/He/She/We/They **might** go to the cinema tonight.
I/You/He/She/We/They **might not** like the film.
It **might** rain tonight.
It **might not** rain tomorrow.

1 Write the sentences in the speech bubbles.

You might not have enough money.
It might rain.
Your teachers might not like it.
I might not have any more children.
You might have an accident.
You might get hungry.

e-ZONE 2 Complete the dialogue with *might* or *might not*.

Bob What's the matter William? Are you worried?
William I've got a job interview at three o'clock in town.
Bob So what's the problem?
William I don't know how to get there.
Bob Well, it's only one o'clock. Why don't you walk?
William I [1] ......might...... get too tired. And then I [2] .... understand the questions in the interview.
Bob OK. Get a taxi.
William It [3] .... be too expensive. I've only got £5 and that [4] .... be enough.
Bob I know. Go by bike.
William Oh no. I [5] .... get there.
Bob Why not?
William I [6] .... have an accident.
Bob OK, so take a bus.
William But I [7] .... get on the wrong bus and I [8] .... get lost.
Bob I give up*. What kind of job is it anyway?
William It's to work with tourist information. Telling people where to go and how to get there.

*__give up__ – aufgeben

3 Match the sentences to the pictures.

1 They might miss the plane.
2 They're going to watch James Bond tonight.
3 They're not going to watch James Bond tonight.
4 They might play tennis.
5 They're going to play tennis.
6 They're not going to play tennis.
7 They might watch James Bond tonight.
8 They're going to miss the plane.
9 They're not going to miss the plane.

4 Complete the sentences with *might*, *be going to* or *not be going to*.

1 The station is 5 km from here so ......we're going to...... take a taxi. It's too far to walk and there's no bus.
2 We .... the opera tonight. I bought the tickets yesterday.
3 I .... buy the red dress or I .... buy the blue one. I can't decide.
4 Jim doesn't eat meat so I'm .... cook steak for them.
5 The children .... sleep at a friend's house this Friday. Great – peace and quiet for us!
6 We .... go to the party. There's a 50% chance.
7 Mum hates loud music so she's .... like this punk CD.
8 We .... have another one. Five children is enough!

5 Write about some of your plans for the weekend.

I'm going to ....
I'm not going to ....
I might ....
I'm going to ....
I'm not going to ....
I might ....

And now go to the e-ZONE and do the Cartoon for Fun!

Past simple (regular and irregular)

Das *past simple* verwendest du, um zu erzählen, was bereits vergangen ist. Fragen bildest du mit **did** und der Grundform des Verbs. Die verneinte Form bildest du mit **didn't** (= **did not**) und der Grundform des Verbs. Achtung: bei **be** (**wasn't**/**weren't**) brauchst du **did**/**didn't** nicht.

Regular verbs	**Irregular verbs**
Statements	
(like) I lik**ed** the film.	(go) I **went** home.
(ask) She ask**ed** a question.	(sing) She **sang** a song at the party.
(try) I tr**ied** to remember.	(be) He **was** there. / They **were** there.
Negation	
(like) I **didn't like** the film.	(go) I **didn't go** home.
(ask) She **didn't ask** a question.	(sing) She **didn't sing** a song at the party.
(try) I **didn't try** to remember.	(be) He **wasn't** there. / They **weren't** there.

1 **Find sixteen past tense forms (↑ ↓ ← →). There are eight regular verbs and eight irregular verbs.**

1 arrived
2 came
3 looked
4 ……………
5 ……………
6 ……………
7 ……………
8 ……………
9 ……………
10 ……………
11 ……………
12 ……………
13 ……………
14 ……………
15 ……………
16 ……………

B	A	R	R	I	V	E	D	D	L	O	I
E	S	A	S	T	C	A	M	E	I	P	D
C	K	N	E	W	W	I	T	H	S	E	E
A	E	R	R	E	D	W	O	L	T	N	T
U	D	F	D	E	N	E	P	O	E	T	D
S	W	O	P	E	A	N	S	O	N	R	E
T	K	P	E	A	R	T	W	K	E	D	K
R	O	L	S	A	W	I	A	E	D	A	L
D	O	D	E	R	A	T	E	D	A	S	A
F	T	A	L	K	E	D	L	O	N	O	W
K	N	I	O	K	L	P	E	D	A	S	W
L	A	U	G	H	E	D	O	S	A	N	G

2 **Complete the puzzle of irregular verbs. What is the secret past simple verb?**

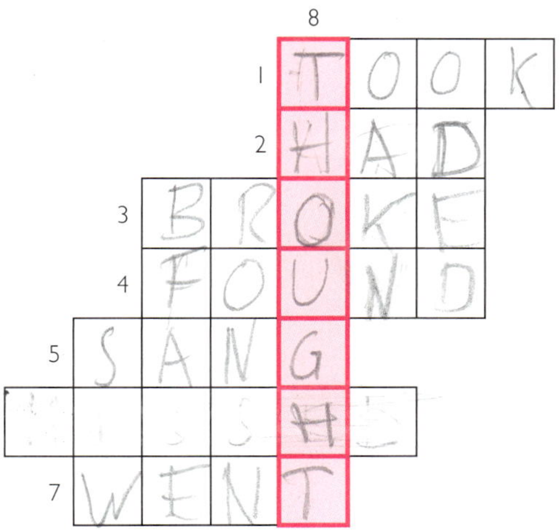

1 Last year we went to Spain – I … lots of photographs.

2 We didn't eat at home last night – we … dinner at a restaurant.

3 He fell off his bicycle and … his leg.

4 I lost my pet mouse yesterday – but I … him under my bed.

5 At the party, some people danced and lots of people … songs.

6 I had to run for the bus – but in the end, I … it!

7 Last year we … to Portugal for our holiday.

8 Oh – Brasilia is the capital of Brazil? I … it was Rio de Janeiro.

3 Complete the tables of past tenses.

verb	past simple	verb	past simple
1 walk	walked	9 take	took
2 arrive	arrived	10 bring	brought
3 dance	danced	11 buy	buyed
4 try	tried	12 sing	sang
5 study	studied	13 laugh	laughed
6 go	went	14 find	found
7 see	saw	15 travel	traveled
8 climb	climbed	16 think	thought

4 Write positive and negative sentences with the past simple. Use the verbs in brackets.

1 (go) Last year, I went to France. I didn't go to Spain.

2 (go) Last week, my dad didn't go to London by plane. He went to the London by train.

3 (meet) On Saturday afternoon, Monica make Sally. She didn't meet Anne.

4 (play) Last Friday, Sam and Ben didn't play tennis. They played ???.

5 (have) This morning, Andy didn't have a shower. He had a bath.

6 (break) Sandra fell off her bike. She broke her arm. She didn't break her leg.

7 (study / meet) Last night, James studied. He didn't meet friends.

8 (go / watch) On Sunday, we didn't go to the cinema. We watched TV.

5 Complete the crossword. The words are in the dialogues.

Alison Saturday I [8]...lost... my bag – my favourite bag! I was really upset.
Brian Did you find it?
Alison Yes, I [7]...found... it yesterday. It was in my bedroom!

Steve I [11]...got... lots of great presents for my birthday last week.
Molly I [1]...thought... your birthday was in April.
Steve No, it was last week. My parents [3]...gave... me a new laptop!

Alex What did you do yesterday?
Mandy I [6↓]...walked... into town.
Alex Did you see anyone?
Mandy Yes, I [9]...saw... Paul. We [6→]...went... to that new café in King Street.
Alex A new café in King Street?
Mandy Yes, it [12]...opened... last month. It's called The Hot Stop. We [2]...had... coffee there.
Alex Was it good?
Mandy No, the coffee was horrible – I [4]...hated... it!

Joanna I'm really angry with you, Simon. You [10]...took... my camera without asking!
Simon Yes, I did. I asked you last week – and you [5]...said... it was OK!
Joanna Really? Last week? OK – then I'm sorry.

		1 T	2 H	O	U	3 G	H	T
	4 H		A			A		
5 S	A	I	D			V		
	T				6 W	E	N	T
	E				A			
	D		7 F		8 L	O	9 S	T
		10 T	O	O	K		A	
11 G			U		E		W	
12 O	P	E	N	E	D			
T			D					

e-ZONE 6 Put the verbs into the past simple tense.

Jack What [1]...did you do... on Saturday?
Hannah I [2]...watched... (watch) the football match on TV.
Jack [3]...Did you like... (like) it?
Hannah No, it [4]...wasn't... (not be) a good match! My team [5]...was... (be) terrible. They [6]...lost... (lose) 3–0.
Jack Oh dear. I'm sorry.
Hannah It's not your fault! But anyway – in the evening we [7]...went... (go) to a nice restaurant for dinner.
Jack We?
Hannah Yes, my parents [8]...took... (take) me and my sister for dinner.
Jack Where [9]...did you go... (go)?
Hannah An Italian place. I [10]...had... (have) some great pasta!
Jack Pasta? I [11]...thought... (think) you didn't like pasta.
Hannah No, I love it! Oh – but I remember, I [12]...said... (say) I didn't like the pasta that my dad makes.
Jack That's right.
Hannah And on Saturday we [13]...didn't want... (not want) dad to make pasta. So we [14]...told... (tell) him to take us out!
Jack Good plan!

7 Complete the sentences. Use the negative form of the verbs in the box.

took
heard
went
~~ate~~
asked
~~liked~~
wrote
found

1 I wasn't very hungry, so I ...didn't eat... much.
2 We watched a film last night but we ...didn't like... it.
3 I left my camera at home, so I ...didn't take... any photographs.
4 My computer's broken, so I ...didn't write... emails last weekend.
5 I was ill yesterday so I ...didn't go... to school.
6 I looked everywhere, but I ...didn't find... my watch.
7 I was happy yesterday because the teacher ...didn't ask... me any questions!
8 I was so tired that I ...didn't hear... my alarm clock this morning – and I was late for school!

e·ZONE 8 Complete the dialogue.

Connor What [1]...did you do... (do) yesterday?
Stuart I [2]...went... (go) into town – and something exciting [3]...happened... (happen)!
Connor What?
Stuart I [4]...found... (find) a wallet on the pavement.
Connor What [5]...did you do... (do)? [6]...Did you open... (open) it?
Stuart Yes, I [7]...opened... (open) it. There [8]...were... (be) more than £100 in it!
Connor [9]...Did you take... (take) the money?
Stuart No, of course I [10]...didn't take... (not take) it. I [11]...took... (take) the wallet to the police station.
Connor [12]...Did... they [13]...ask... (ask) you lots of questions?
Stuart No. They [14]...got... (get) the name of the owner from his driving licence and they [15]...phoned... (phone) him. He [16]...came... (come) to the police station and [17]...got... (get) his wallet.
Connor [18]...Was... (be) he happy?
Stuart Yes. He [19]...said... (say) thank you and he [20]...gave... (give) me £10.

And now go to the e·ZONE and do the Cartoon for Fun!

Past time expressions

1 Complete the words in the sentences.

1 We did some shopping and had a coffee.
T h e n we went home.

2 My uncle's staying with us. He arrived three days a g o .

3 We sat down in the cinema and two minutes l a t e r the film started.

4 The film was awful! A f t e r half an hour, we left.

5 Last summer we were in Italy. O n e day, we went to Venice.
The n e x t day, we visited Padua.

6 I waited for Julie for an hour. F i n a l l y, she arrived and said she was sorry.

e·ZONE **2 Replace the underlined words with the correct object pronouns.**

ten minutes later
~~One day~~
~~Two years ago~~
~~The next day~~
~~finally~~
~~After thirty minutes~~

1 Two years ago, my family (my mum and dad, my little brother Jeremy and me) went on holiday to London. 2 The next day, we went out to look in some shops. We went to Oxford Street and started walking around. There were hundreds of people everywhere. Suddenly, my mum asked: 'Where's Jeremy?' Well, we looked everywhere for him but we couldn't find him. 3 After thirty minutes, my dad said: 'I'm going to the police.' So we all went to the police station. We walked in, and my dad started to say what the problem was. My mum was really worried – but, 4 ten minutes later, a policewoman came in and she was holding Jeremy's hand. 'We found him in a toyshop,' the policewoman said. Mum was so happy! I was happy too, because 5 finally we could go and finish our shopping!

6 One day, Jeremy said 'Let's go shopping again.' My parents just said: 'Noooo!!'

And now go to the e·ZONE and do the Cartoon for Fun!

some / any

Wenn du dich auf Dinge beziehst, die du nicht zählen kannst, oder von denen du nicht weißt wieviele es sind, verwendest du **some**.
Du verwendest **any**, wenn du fragen willst, ob es etwas gibt, oder sagen willst, dass etwas nicht vorhanden ist.

some	any
We've got **some onions**.	We haven't got **any onions**.
I've got **some money**.	I haven't got **any money**.
Do you want **some potatoes**?	Is there **any milk** in the fridge?
Would you like **some soup**?	Have we got **any strawberries**?

e·ZONE **1 Match the sentences / questions with the pictures.**

1 Dad – can I have some money, please?
2 Mum – have we got any milk?
3 Mum – we need some ice cream.
4 No thanks – I don't want any ice cream.
5 Of course I can go out – I haven't got any work!
6 Sis – I need to buy something. Have you got any money?
7 Sorry, I can't go out – I've got to do some work.
8 Would you like some milk?

2 Match the sentences to make mini-dialogues.

1 We haven't got any chocolate.
2 Let's listen to some music.
3 Hello. Do you need any help?
4 I haven't got any ideas.
5 Have you got any pets at home?
6 Mum – we haven't got any toothpaste.
7 Please be quiet – I've got some work to do.
8 Oh no – there are some dogs in the street.

a Yes please – I want some information about buses.
b Look in the cupboard – there's some toothpaste in there.
c OK – I'm not going to make any noise.
d Yes we have – there's some in the kitchen.
e No – I'd prefer to watch some DVDs.
f Where? I can't see any dogs!
g No – mum doesn't want any animals in the house.
h There are some books here – perhaps there are some ideas in them.

3 Put the words in the correct order.

1 help / any / Do / need / you ?
Do you need any help?

2 information / like / some / about / I'd / concerts .
I'd like some information about concerts.

3 please / Can / some / some / eggs / and / I / have / cheese ?
Can I have some eggs and some cheese please?

4 yoghurt / there / in / Is / fridge / the / any ?
Is there any yoghurt in the fridge?

5 fun / out / have / and / Let's / some / go .
Let's go out and have some fun.

6 medicine / going / buy / for my cold / some / to / I'm .
I'm going to buy some medicine for my cold.

4 Write the phrases in the correct places.

~~any money~~
~~some money~~
~~any kids~~
~~some kids~~
~~any examples~~
~~some examples~~

1 I don't understand this very well – the teacher didn't give us ......any examples...... .

2 It's free! You don't need ......any money...... to get in.

3 Sorry – you have to be over 18! We don't want ......any kids...... in here.

4 It's a difficult bit of grammar. We need ......some examples...... to help us.

5 There were ......some kids...... at the shopping mall, but I didn't know them.

6 My parents gave me ......some money...... for my birthday, so I'm going to buy something nice.

5 Look at the picture. Write sentences.

1 cars There are some cars.

2 bicycles There aren't any bicycles.

3 kids There aren't any kids.

4 dogs There are some dogs.

5 cats There aren't any cats.

6 shops There are some shops.

e-ZONE 6 Complete the mini-dialogues with *some* or *any*.

1 **A** Have you got ......any...... CDs I can listen to?
B Yes – I've got ......some...... CDs here in my backpack. Here you are.

2 **A** Mum – I've got ......some...... problems with my homework.
B Sorry dear – I haven't got ......any...... time right now. Talk to me later.

3 **A** We need ......some...... information about her for our project.
B Well, I looked on the Internet but I didn't find ......any...... information at all.

4 **A** The teacher didn't give us ......any...... homework tonight.
B Yes she did! She gave us ......some...... grammar exercises to do.

5 **A** Let's go to the supermarket. We need to buy ......some...... food.
B OK, but don't forget we need ......some...... money to buy things!

And now go to the e-ZONE and do the Cartoon for Fun!

Irregular plurals

Unregelmäßige Pluralformen solltest du dir immer gemeinsam mit der Singularform des Nomen einprägen.

one car – two car**s**
one child – two child**ren** (not two ~~childs~~)

1 Write the words under the pictures.

child
teeth
children
foot
tooth
people
feet
goose
person
~~geese~~
woman
women

1 geese

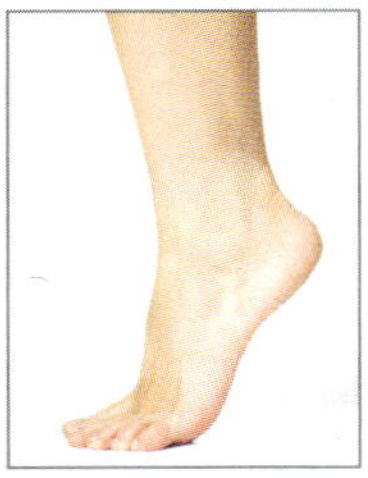
2 foot

3 women

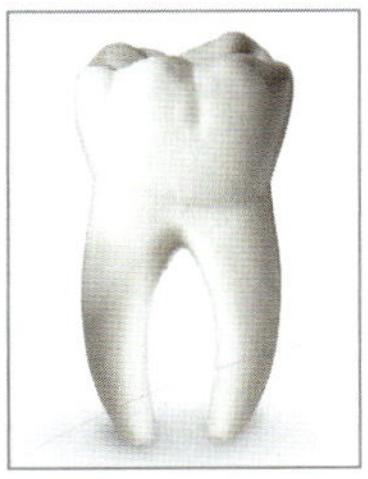
4 tooth

5 goose

6 child

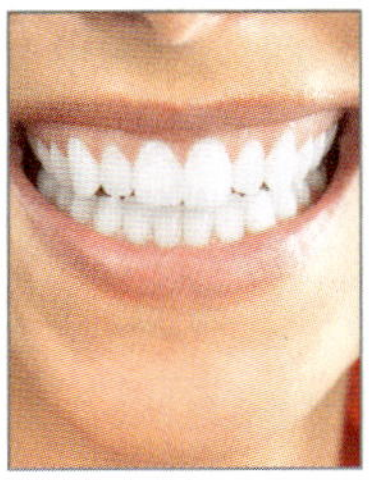
7 teeth

8 children

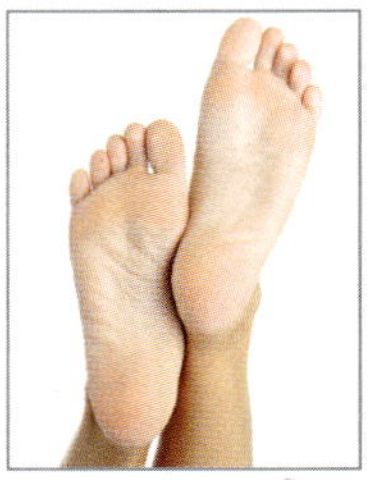
9 feet

10 people

11 person

12 woman

2 Write the plurals of the following words.

1 man – men
2 knife – knives
3 thief – thieves
4 leaf – leaves
5 fish – fish
6 sheep – sheep

3 Use words from 1 and 2 to complete the mini-dialogues.

1 **A** Did you have a good time fishing?
B Yes, but I only caught two fish .

2 **A** I love autumn.
B Me too. The Leaves on the trees are really beautiful colours.

3 **A** Why are you walking like that?
B Because my right foot hurts.

4 **A** Is that a duck?
B No, it's a goose .

5 **A** Why are you going to the dentists?
B Because my tooth fell out. Look – here it is.

6 **A** Be careful with that knife . It's very sharp.
B Ow! Too late.

7 **A** How many children do you want?
B Two, a boy and a girl.

8 **A** Did the police catch the thieves?
B They only caught one of them.

Questions with *who*

Wenn du fragen möchtest, wer etwas macht, verwendest du das Fragewort **who** zusammen mit dem passenden Verb in der dritten Person singular. Du musst natürlich auch auf die richtige Zeitform achten!

1 Match the questions with the picture answers.

1 Who plays Captain Jack Sparrow in *Pirates of the Caribbean*?
2 Who wrote *Romeo and Juliet*?
3 Who won the 2010 world cup?
4 Who is a comedy film star?
5 Who lives in Buckingham Palace?
6 Who became the President of the USA in 2008?

a

b

c

e

d

f

2 Write the questions for the answers.

1 **A** Who told you?
B Brian (told me).

2 **A** Who sent you the valentine card?
B I don't know (who sent me the valentine card).

3 **A** Who Paid for my new computer?
B Dad (paid for my new computer).

4 **A** Who watch another DVD?
B I want to (watch another DVD).

5 **A** Who called the police?
B I'm not sure (who called the police).

e·ZONE **3 Put the words in order to make questions.**

1 Batman / Who / the / plays / new
Who plays the new Batman?

2 song / Who / this / sings
Who sings this song?

3 wants / eat / to / now / Who
Who wants to eat now?

4 that / you / lovely / gave / Who / jumper
Who gave you that lovely jumper?

5 you / last / phoned / night / Who
Who phoned you last night?

4 Match the questions in 3 with the answers.

1 My gran. It was a birthday present. [4]
2 I'm not sure but it might be *U2*. [2]
3 Jo. She had a question about the homework. [5]
4 I do. I'm really hungry. [3]
5 Christian Bale. [1]

And now go to the e·ZONE and do the Cartoon for Fun!

like (doing)

So drückst du aus, ob jemand eine Tätigkeit mag oder nicht mag.

Samantha **doesn't like reading** but she **likes listening** to music.
James **likes running** but he **doesn't like swimming**.

e-ZONE **1 Write the verbs in brackets in the correct form.**

1 My brother loves ...listening... to music. (listen)
2 My sister doesn't like .... (sing)
3 All of us like .... (read)
4 Our cat likes .... trees. (climb)
5 I don't like .... television. (watch)
6 My mother and father like .... (dance)
7 Do you like .... shopping? (go)
8 I love .... photographs. (take)

2 Look at the information. Write sentences about the people.

😍 = love 🙂 = like ☹ = not like 😣 = hate

			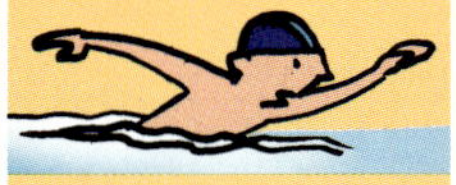	
Pete	😣	😍	🙂	☹
Sarah	☹	😣	😍	🙂
Andy and Sue	🙂	☹	😣	😍

1 Pete ...loves reading. He likes swimming but he doesn't like talking on the phone. He hates shopping!...
2 Sarah ....
3 Andy and Sue ....

3 Now write about you. Write about the things in 2. Then say four other things you *love / like / don't like / hate* doing!

I .... going shopping.
I .... reading.
I .... swimming.
I .... talking on the phone.
I love ....
I like ....
I don't like ....
I hate ....

And now go to the e-ZONE and do the Cartoon for Fun!

must / mustn't

Hello! See me on the e·ZONE to discover more about *must / mustn't* and to learn better when to use it.

So drückst du aus, ob jemand etwas tun muss oder nicht tun darf. Achtung: **mustn't** bedeutet im Deutschen „nicht dürfen" und nicht „nicht müssen".

You **must be** home before ten.
I **mustn't be** late for school.
We **must switch** our phones off.
You **mustn't feed** the animals in the zoo.

1 Match the person and the things he/she says.

1 You mustn't feed the animals.
2 You mustn't come home late.
3 You mustn't walk on the grass.
4 You must be quiet in here.
5 You must clean your teeth two or three times a day.
6 You must eat fruit and vegetables.

a doctor
b librarian*
c dentist
d zoo-keeper
e park-keeper
f parent

***librarian** – Bibliothekar/in

2 Complete the sentences.

The Wannagobak campsite has lots of rules. Here they are:

1 You ......mustn't play...... loud music.
2 You .... at 6 o'clock.
3 You .... your clothes on the tent-ropes.
4 You .... on the campsite.
5 You .... at 10 o'clock.
6 You .... the campsite.

e·ZONE 3 Complete the sentences. Use *must* or *mustn't* and a verb from the box.

~~be~~
eat
climb
be
jump
put
wear
touch

1 The baby's asleep, so you ......must be...... quiet, OK?
2 Come on – it's 8.30 already. We .... late for school again!
3 It's an important day, so you .... your best clothes.
4 Your shoes are very dirty – you .... them on the chairs.
5 Hamburgers aren't good for you, so you .... too many.
6 Now remember – in the museum, you can look but you .... anything!
7 An important rule in the swimming pool is – you .... into the pool.
8 Snowy – you silly cat! You .... trees if you can't get down again!

And now go to the e·ZONE and do the Cartoon for Fun!

Adverbs of manner

Hiermit kannst du die Art und Weise beschreiben, wie jemand etwas macht.
Bildung: Adjektiv + **ly**
Achtung: **y** wird zu **i** + **ly**;
e wird vor dem **ly** weggelassen.
Leider gibt es auch ein paar Ausnahmen, die du lernen solltest!

Talk quiet**ly**.
She smiled happ**ily**.
He sings really **well**.

1 Find 10 adverbs and write them in the 2nd column in the table. (Look ↑ ↓ ← →.)

I	N	T	E	L	L	I	G	E	N	T	L	Y	K
E	U	A	A	Q	S	K	H	F	U	G	K	L	N
G	J	E	S	E	P	O	F	H	G	F	A	S	T
N	E	R	I	T	E	E	J	B	F	K	L	U	B
J	H	F	L	H	N	A	Z	N	S	V	M	O	S
Y	G	D	Y	J	K	N	Y	E	E	W	G	R	R
L	M	Y	L	T	H	G	I	R	B	Y	N	E	E
S	P	O	C	H	B	R	R	V	D	L	C	G	N
U	Y	S	Q	U	T	I	E	O	G	R	Y	N	B
O	T	F	D	M	Y	L	L	U	F	E	R	A	C
I	B	S	R	M	S	Y	K	S	R	V	Q	D	H
R	U	T	Z	P	A	L	U	L	O	E	I	S	T
U	W	N	O	Z	U	G	H	Y	T	L	K	L	P
F	K	P	L	Y	K	L	U	Z	D	C	D	J	R

adjective	adverb
intelligent	intelligently

2 Write the adjectives and complete the first column in the table in 1.

3 Write the adverbs for the adjectives.

angry – angrily; boring – ……; good – ……; excited – ……
bad – ……; happy – ……; fast – ……; easy – ……
clever – ……; tired – ……; serious – ……; terrible – ……

4 Find the opposites.

~~jokingly~~ badly well
slowly terribly quietly
brilliantly happily quickly
loudly sadly ~~seriously~~

jokingly – seriously
…… – ……
…… – ……
…… – ……
…… – ……
…… – ……

e-ZONE **5** **Underline the correct adverb.**

1 I did really *badly* / *dangerously* / *cleverly* in the test. I got 25%!
2 He shouted at us *boringly* / *jokingly* / *furiously*. He wasn't happy at all!
3 He passed his driving test *intelligently* / *easily* / *fast*. He had no problems.
4 The stars shone *quietly* / *slowly* / *brightly* in the sky.
5 'I've won the lottery!' he told us *cleverly* / *sadly* / *excitedly*.
6 He speaks Italian *dangerously* / *nervously* / *brilliantly*. He's like an Italian.
7 He ran really *slowly* / *furiously* / *fast* and won the race.
8 He did his homework *boringly* / *carefully* / *jokingly* and made no mistakes.

6 **Look at the underlined word. Write adverb or adjective.**

1 We walked slowly to school. – ....adverb........
2 It was a beautiful Monday morning. – ....
3 Don't get close to that dog. It's dangerous. – ....
4 The dog barked at us furiously. – ....
5 She speaks French very well. – ....
6 She always gets good grades in her French tests. – ....
7 That was a difficult question. – ....
8 I think he answered that question very intelligently. – ....

e-ZONE **7** **Complete the sentences with the adverbs in the box.**

angrily
dangerously
loudly
happily
carefully
~~brightly~~
quietly
furiously

1 It's a normal Monday morning. The sun is shining ....brightly........ .
2 Inside the classroom, Mr Lame is talking ....
3 Nobody is listening. Dan is whispering .... into May's ear.
4 Kevin is smiling .... at Betty.
5 Betty is looking .... at Kevin.
6 Only Emily is listening .... She's Mr Lame's favourite.
7 Steve is sitting on his chair ....
8 Now Mr Lame is shouting .... Yes, it's a normal Monday morning.

8 How do these people speak? Follow the lines to find out and then write sentences.

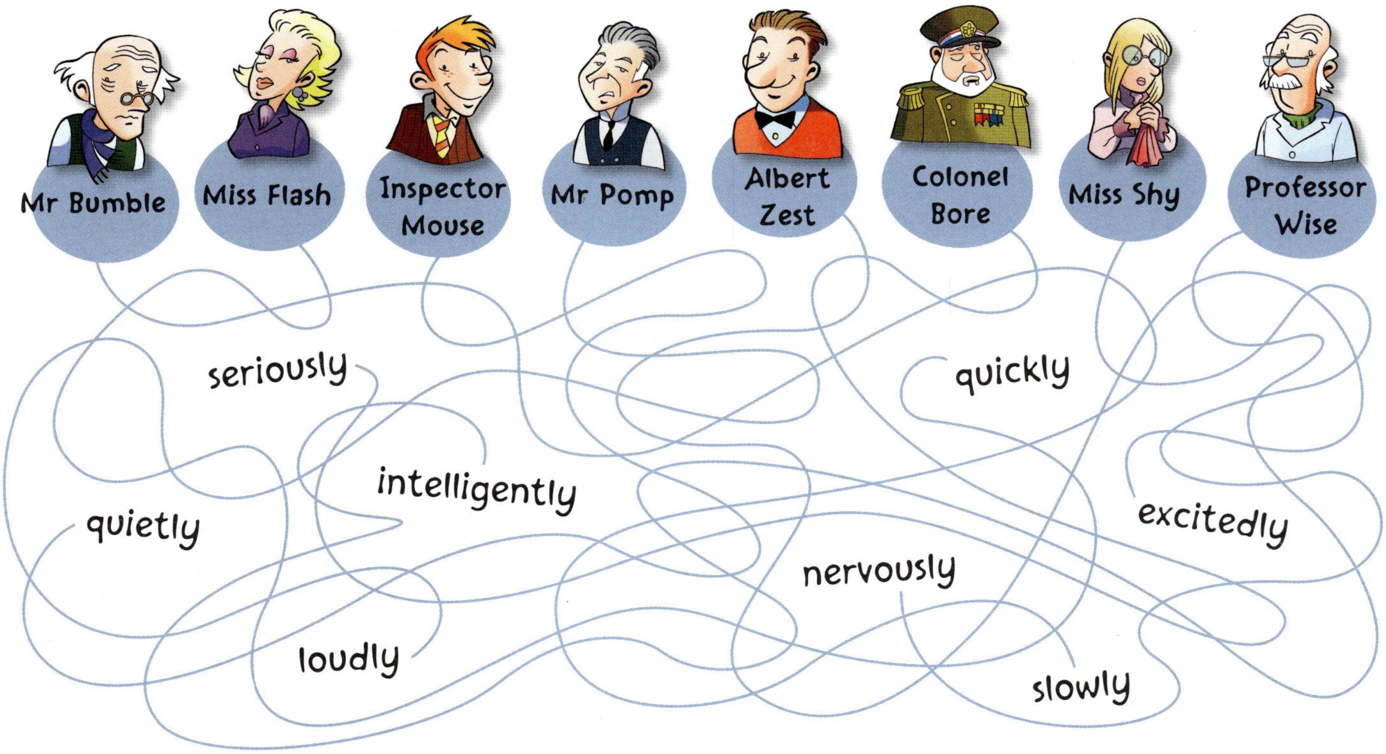

1 Mr Bumble speaks slowly .
2 Miss Flash ....
3 Inspector Mouse ....
4 Mr Pomp ....
5 Albert Zest ....
6 Colonel Bore ....
7 Miss Shy ....
8 Professor Wise ....

9 Read the beginning of the story and underline the correct words.

Mr Bumble was a [1] *rich / richly* man but not anymore because Mr Bumble was dead. Mr Bumble had nothing now but a [2] *sharp / sharply* knife in his back. Inspector Mouse looked [3] *careful / carefully* at the body. Then he turned around [4] *quick / quickly* and spoke [5] *excited / excitedly* to his friend Albert Zest. This was unusual because Inspector Mouse usually spoke [6] *quiet / quietly* but at this moment he was very [7] *excited / excitedly*.

'This knife did not kill Mr Bumble.' He said. 'Look at these [8] *bright / brightly* spots around his mouth. Cyanide killed him!'

'But who gave him the poison?' asked Zest.

'That is what I need to find out [9] *quick / quickly*.' Replied the Inspector 'And I am going to need your help young man. There were five people in the house yesterday afternoon at the time of the murder. They were all there to celebrate Mr Bumble's 80th birthday tomorrow. We need to talk [10] *serious / seriously* with all of them.'

10 Read the next part of the story and complete with the adverbs of the adjectives.

Inspector Mouse looked [1] carefully (careful) at his notes and told Albert Zest about the suspects.

"Colonel Bore is an old army friend of Mr Bumble. He reacted* [2] .... (bad) when I told him about the murder. He was very sad. He also has a good alibi because he wasn't at the house all afternoon. He was in the village visiting an aunt. And there are lots of witnesses who saw him driving his Rolls Royce [3] .... (slow) along the roads."

"I didn't like Mr Pomp. He spoke [4] .... (rude) to me and didn't want to help at all. He's Mr Bumble's secretary. He organised the weekend and invited everyone to the party. When I asked him why he wanted Mr Bumble dead, he reacted [5] .... (angry) and told me he hasn't got a job any more."

"Miss Shy is an interesting woman. She met Mr Bumble on the Internet. They both enjoy bird-watching and spent weekends away together. When I asked her about romance she reacted [6] .... (furious). I don't think she liked my question."

"Professor Wise is chemistry professor at London university. He's very well-educated and can talk [7] .... (intelligent) about anything. He's an old school friend of Mr Bumble. He says he saw Colonel Bore shouting [8] .... (loud) with Mr Bumble about half an hour before the murder."

"Miss Flash spoke [9] .... (nervous) when I asked her questions. But she's a nervous person so maybe that's not a very important fact. She knew Mr Bumble [10] .... (good) because she worked for him for forty years."

So Zest. What do you think? Do you know who our murderer is?

***react** – reagieren

11 Who do you think the murderer is? Read the solution at the bottom of the page.

12 Rewrite the sentences to include the words.

1 He did his homework but he still made a mistake. (carefully / big)

He did his homework carefully but he still made a big mistake.

2 It was a Maths test and I finished. (easy / quickly)

....

3 I walked because I had a bag. (slowly / heavy)

....

4 It was a summer day and the sun shone. (lovely / brightly)

....

5 I had to talk because it was a party. (loudly / noisy)

....

6 The children got up and opened their presents. (early / excitedly)

....

7 My dad drove and we were all passengers. (dangerously / nervous)

....

8 It was a song and she sang it. (brilliant / well)

....

13 Answer the questions about you.

How do you:

1 talk?

I talk quickly.

2 walk?

....

3 do your homework?

....

4 speak English?

....

5 dance?

....

6 open birthday presents?

....

7 cook?

....

8 play tennis?

....

Professor Wise is the murderer. He says he saw Colonel Bore shouting with Mr Bumble just before the murder. Bore has an alibi for the afternoon so Wise is lying. Also because he is a Chemistry professor he can easily get hold of cyanide.

And now go to the e-ZONE and do the Cartoon for Fun!

whose + possessive 's

So kannst du fragen und angeben, wem etwas gehört.

Whose is this bag? It's Kevin'**s** (bag). It's Doris' (bag).

e·ZONE **1 Write the answers to the questions. Use the names in the box to help you.**

Spiderman
Harry Potter
Mickey Mouse
Superman
Batman
~~James Bond~~
Marge Simpson
Sherlock Holmes

1 Whose is this codename?
It's James Bond's codename.

2 Whose is this car?
....

3 Whose is this ear?
....

4 Whose is this cape?
....

5 Whose is this mask?
....

6 Whose is this pipe?
....

7 Whose is this wand?
....

8 Whose is this hair?
....

2 Look at the picture and write dialogues about the objects.

1
A *Whose are these earrings?*
B *They're Kerry's earrings.*

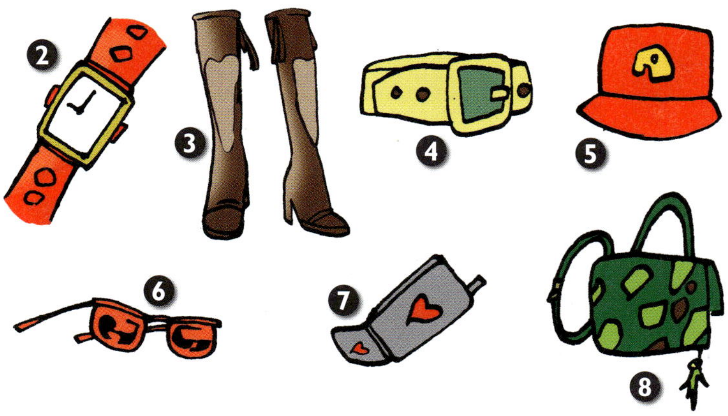

And now go to the e·ZONE and do the Cartoon for Fun!

Possessive pronouns

So kannst du sagen, dass dir oder jemand anderem etwas gehört.

1 Complete the table with the words in the box.

ours	hers
~~his~~	his
theirs	yours
your	~~my~~
their	our
mine	her

I	That's ......my...... bike.	That's ....
You	That's .... bike.	That's ....
He	That's .... bike.	That's ......his...... .
She	That's .... bike.	That's ....
We	That's .... bike.	That's ....
They	That's .... bike.	That's ....

2 Choose the correct option.

1. Don't worry. It's not <u>*your*</u> / *yours* problem.
2. It not your problem. It's *her* / *hers*.
3. Excuse me. That pizza. I think it's *our* / *ours*.
4. Don't eat it. It's *their* / *theirs*.
5. This is where we live. This is *our* / *ours* home.
6. *Their* / *Theirs* dog is really ugly.
7. These are my shoes and those are *your* / *yours*.
8. I really like *her* / *hers* trousers.

3 Follow the lines. Complete the sentences with the correct possessive pronoun.

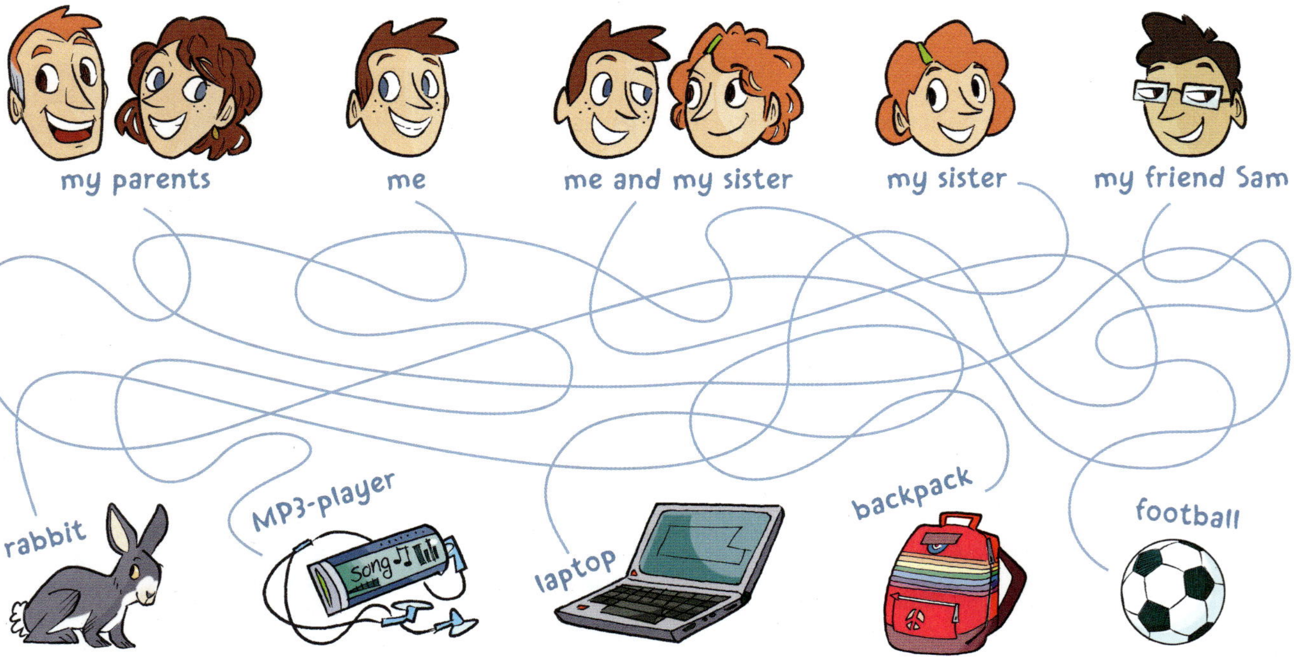

1. My parents: The ....laptop.......... is ....
2. My sister and me: The .... is ....
3. My sister: The .... is ....
4. My friend Sam: The .... is ....
5. Me: The .... is ....

4 Complete the sentences with the missing pronouns.

e·ZONE 5 Complete the dialogues with the missing words.

Teacher Hi Mike, someone left this scarf in the classroom. Is it [1]....yours....?

Mike No it's not [2].................... scarf. Ask Bill. I think it's [3].................... .

(Two minutes later.)

Teacher Bill, is this [4].................... scarf?

Bill Let me have a look. No, it's not [5].................... . It might be Jane's scarf. Ask [6].................... .

(Two minutes later.)

Teacher Jane? Is this [7]....................?

Jane No, sir. I think it's the twins'.

Teacher Richard and Henry? So, is it [8].................... scarf?

Jane Yes, I think it's [9].................... .

(Two minutes later.)

Teacher Richard, Henry. Is this [10]....................?

Twins No, it's not [11].................... .

Teacher [12].................... scarf is it?

Henry Can I have a look at it?

Teacher Sure. Here you are.

Henry It's got the initials* KL. Aren't those [13].................... initials, sir?

Teacher Yes, they're [14].................... initials.

Henry I think this is [15].................... scarf, sir.

Teacher Oh yes. It is. It's [16].................... .

***initials** – Anfangsbuchstaben

And now go to the e·ZONE and do the Cartoon for Fun!

Past participles

Das *past participle* oder die „dritte Form" eines Verbs brauchst du, um das *present perfect* zu bilden. Es gibt regelmäßige und unregelmäßige Formen. Bei regelmäßigen Verben hängst du **–ed** oder **–d** an die Grundform an.

Regular			**Irregular**		
Infinitive	**Past Simple**	**Past Participle**	**Infinitive**	**Past Simple**	**Past Participle**
pass	pass**ed**	pass**ed**	go	went	**gone**
walk	walk**ed**	walk**ed**	see	saw	**seen**
move	mov**ed**	mov**ed**	come	came	**come**
talk	talk**ed**	talk**ed**	cut	cut	**cut**

1 Find twelve past participles in the wordsnake.

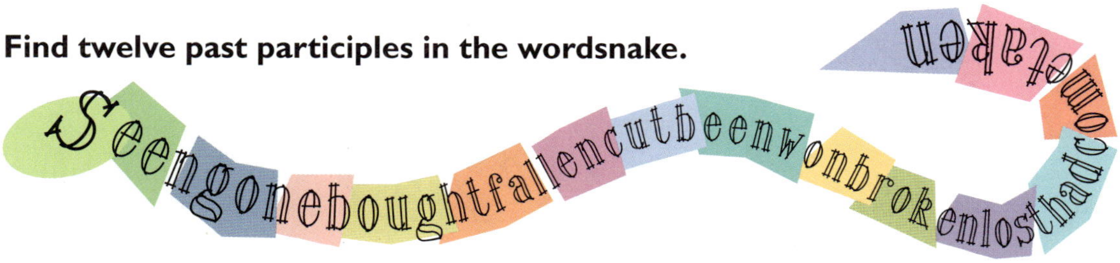

2 Write the words from 1 in the correct places to complete the table.

1 go	went	gone	**7** win	won	....
2 see	saw	....	**8** break	broke	....
3 come	came	....	**9** buy	bought	....
4 cut	cut	....	**10** fall	fell	....
5 be	was/were	....	**11** lose	lost	....
6 take	took	....	**12** have	had	....

3 Use a word from 1 to complete each sentence.

1 Look! Inspector Groans has fallen out a tree again!
2 I'm not hungry, thanks – I've .... lunch.
3 John's not here – he's .... into town to do some shopping.
4 Look – I've .... three new CDs. Do you want to listen to them?
5 I'm really happy because my team has .... the championship!
6 There's blood on my finger – I think I've .... it.
7 We've only been here two days, and my sister has .... 100 photographs already!
8 Do you know where my book is? I've .... it!

Present perfect

Hello! See me on the e-ZONE to discover more about the *present perfect* and to learn better when to use it.

Das *present perfect* verwendest du, wenn du sagen willst, dass etwas gerade oder vor kurzer Zeit passiert ist. Dabei gibst du keinen genauen Zeitpunkt an.

I/You/We/They**'ve bought** (= **have bought**) a new pair of shoes.
He/She/It**'s been** (= **has been**) here a long time.

I/You/We/They **haven't** (= **have not**) **bought** a new pair of shoes.
He/She/It **hasn't** (= **has not**) **been** here a long time.

Have I/you/we/they **eaten** too much?
Has he/she/it **been** here a long time?

1 Write the sentences using short forms.

1 We have not been here before.
We haven't been here before.
2 It has not rained for a long time.
....
3 I have bought a new book.
....
4 My parents have not seen this film.
....
5 He has always worked here.
....
6 We have not eaten our lunch.
....
7 You have listened to all my CDs.
....
8 My favourite band has made a new CD.
....

e-ZONE 2 Match the pictures and the sentences.

1 I've won!
2 He's lost his glasses.
3 They haven't had their dinner.
4 We've been to the shops.
5 I think I've broken my leg.
6 I've seen it – it's really good.
7 He's fallen off his bike.
8 She's swum 3 kilometres.

3 Make the sentences negative.

1 I've bought a new laptop. I haven't bought a new laptop.
2 We've moved house. ....
3 They've come back from their holiday. ....
4 I've studied for tomorrow's test. ....
5 My dad's made dinner. ....

4 Match the sentences to make mini-dialogues.

1 Where are your glasses?
2 Is Jenny here?
3 Would you like some more?
4 Why does she know so much about Italy?
5 Is your dog ill?
6 Your mum speaks good French, doesn't she?
7 Is *High School Musical* your favourite film?
8 Why don't you phone him?
9 Someone told me that your mother's a writer.
10 You look very happy.
11 I phoned you last night – no answer.
12 Why isn't Tom here?

a She's been there about ten times!
b Yes. I think it's eaten something bad.
c I can't – I've lost his number.
d Yes. She's written about six books.
e I don't know. I've lost them.
f He's gone to Italy on holiday.
g No, she's gone to see her friend Amy.
h I am. I've had some good news!
i Yes, she does. She's lived in Paris.
j Yeah, sorry – I've lost my mobile phone.
k No, I've eaten lots, thank you.
l Yes, I've seen it about ten times!

e-ZONE

5 Read the dialogue. Put the verbs into the correct form of the present perfect.

A You look tired.
B I am. I [1] 've been .... (be) very busy.
A Oh? What [2] .... you .... (do)?
B Well, I [3] .... (tidy) my room.
A Good – it was terrible before! And ...?
B And I [4] .... (do) my homework.
A Excellent. [5] .... you .... (feed) the hamster?
B No – the hamster isn't hungry. But I [6] .... (clean) its cage.
A Well, you're right – you [7] .... (be) busy! Just one more question.
B Yes?
A [8] .... you .... (cook) dinner for us?
B Mum – give me a break*!

*__give me a break__ – lass mich in Ruhe

6 Put the words in order to make sentences and questions.

1 gone / America / My / to / has / dad
My dad has gone to America.
2 me / hasn't / phoned / Timothy
....
3 windsurfing / I've / three times / been
....
4 countries / I've / to / different / travelled / of / lots
....
5 this / times / read / book / I've / four
....
6 all / eaten / chocolate / has / Tess / the
....
7 their / Have / CD / new / you / heard / ?
....
8 homework / the / Has / us / given / any / teacher / ?
....

7 Complete with the words in the box.

climbed
found
learned
made
swum
~~travelled~~
taken
walked
written

In my life …

I've 1 ……travelled…… round the world.

I've 2 ……………… lots of mountains.

I've 3 ……………… in lakes and rivers.

I've 4 ……………… across deserts.

I've 5 ……………… thousands of photographs.

I've 6 ……………… lots of new friends.

I've 7 ……………… twenty languages.

I've 8 ……………… a hundred poems.

But … I haven't 9 ……………… a man to love!

8 Complete the sentences. Use the present perfect form of the verbs in the box.

eat
not learn
not open
see
travel
~~play~~
work
win
not write
not listen

1 I'm bored with this game now – I ……'ve played…… it hundreds of times!

2 I've got some new CDs, but I ……………… to them.

3 I ……………… Indian food lots of times.

4 Uncle James sent me a birthday present – but I ……………… it yet.

5 It's a nice film, but I ……………… much better ones.

6 My aunt Jessica ……………… to more than fifteen different countries!

7 He's my favourite tennis player – he ……………… Wimbledon six times!

8 I love cars, but I ……………… how to drive.

9 My dad ……………… for more than ten different companies.

10 I wrote an email to my friend, but she ……………… back to me.

e·ZONE

9 Put the verbs into the present perfect.

One of my friends at school is Dilap. His parents are from India – they came to Britain twenty-five years ago. They live in the same street as me – they 1 ……'ve…… always ……lived…… (live) in the same house. Dilap and I went to the same junior school and we 2 ……………… (be) friends since then.

Dilap's really smart. He plays chess and he's very good – he 3 ……………… (win) lots of school tournaments. He 4 ……………… (beat) the chess teacher lots of times, too! He's also really good at Maths and at Information Technology. Dilap says that people from India 5 ……………… always ……………… (be) good with computers and things like that. He 6 ……………… (try) to teach me things about IT, but he 7 ……………… never ……………… (be) very successful!

Dilap 8 ……………… (visit) India about six times, I think – his family goes back every year to see their relatives. He 9 ……………… always ……………… (enjoy) the visits to India, he says. I'd love to go with him one day – but so far, he 10 ……………… (not invite) me!

And now go to the e·ZONE and do the Cartoon for Fun!

Present perfect + *already* / *yet*

Wenn du sagen möchtest, dass jemand etwas schon gemacht hat, verwendest du das *present perfect* zusammen mit dem Wort **already**.

Wenn du sagen möchtest, dass jemand etwas noch nicht gemacht hat, verwendest du das *present perfect* zusammen mit den Wörtern **not yet**.

I**'ve already** washed the car.
We**'ve already** seen this film.
I **haven't done** my homework **yet**.
She **hasn't told** him **yet**.

e-ZONE **1** **Match the pictures with sentences.**

1 He's already had a shower.
2 He hasn't had a shower yet.
3 We've already eaten.
4 We haven't eaten yet.
5 He hasn't caught a fish yet.
6 He's already caught two fish.
7 He hasn't fed the dog yet.
8 He's already fed the dog.

e-ZONE **2** **Complete the newspaper article with the phrases in the box.**

already competed
US yet
already attracted
already broken
18 yet
~~already won~~
already earned
gold medal yet

Welcome to Nathan Holmes

Britain's newest star in the swimming pool

He's [1] already won the 100 m and 200 m freestyle British championship. And he's [2] .... the UK record at both these distances. And he's not even turned [3] .... He only does that in November.

He's [4] .... all over Europe but he hasn't swum in the [5] ....

Next year he starts training in LA. It's a dream come true.

He's [6] .... more than £100,000 in prize money. And the really big money is going to come soon because he's [7] .... the interest of some very important companies.

And his biggest dream of all – the Olympics. He hasn't won an Olympic [8] .... But we're sure he's going to win one soon.

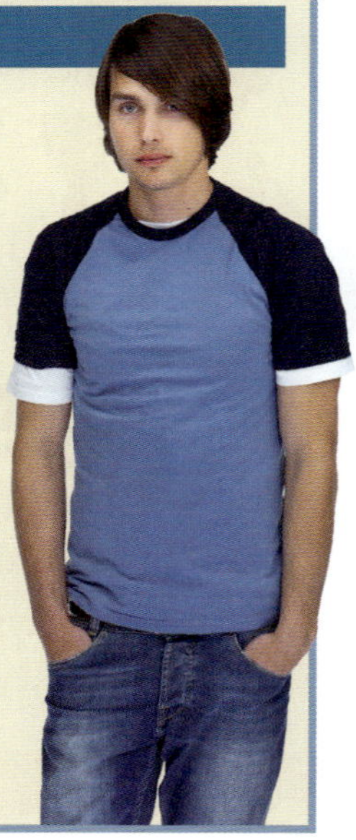

3 Write the sentences using short forms.

1 I have not seen this film yet.
I haven't seen this film yet.

2 She has not spoken to me yet.
....

3 Henry has already written the email.
....

4 I have already asked my mum.
....

5 My dad has already found a new job.
....

6 They have not invited me to their party yet.
....

7 You have already told me that.
....

8 We have not finished our lunch yet.
....

4 Complete the sentences with the present perfect forms of the verbs.

1 She ......'s...... already ......bought...... a new dress but no one ......'s...... ......invited...... her to the party yet. (buy / invite)

2 He .... to play the guitar yet but he .... already .... an expensive guitar. (not learn / get)

3 She .... already .... the washing-up but we .... dinner yet. (do / not finish)

4 I .... you the question yet but you .... already .... me your answer. (not ask / give)

5 I .... that film yet but he .... already .... me the end of it. (not see / tell)

6 You .... already .... off your coat but the rain .... yet. (take / not stop)

7 She .... already .... on the lights but it .... dark yet. (turn / not get)

8 He .... his computer yet and he .... already .... it. (not use / break)

e-ZONE 5 Complete the dialogue with *yet* or *already*.

Tim Come on Paul, let's go.
Paul I'm not ready [1]......yet...... .
Tim What! But the film starts in half an hour.
Paul That's OK. I've [2].................. ordered a taxi for 7.30.
Tim 7.30! The film starts at 7.45!
Paul So what's the problem?
Tim The problem is that we haven't got our tickets [3].................. .
Paul Yes we have.
Tim We have?
Paul I've [4].................. told you twice.
Tim So tell me again.
Paul I've [5].................. bought our tickets. I got them online.

Tim Online. Look, here they are. Two tickets for *The Final Conflict*.
Paul *The Final Conflict*! But I've [6].................. seen *The Final Conflict*!
Tim Whoops!

6 **Write the questions and then match them with the answers below.**

1 you / phone / Carl
Have you phoned Carl yet?

2 you / play / Kingdom of Doom
..............................?

3 you / sell / your computer
..............................?

4 you / fix / your bike
..............................?

5 she / invite / you to her party
..............................?

6 she / give / you a birthday present
..............................?

7 he / do / the washing-up
..............................?

8 he / finish / the book
..............................?

a Yes, he did it straight after dinner.

b No, it's still broken.

c No, I think she's forgotten.

d I think he's on the last chapter.

e I tried but he didn't answer.

f No. No one wants to buy it.

g I got to level 2 and I gave up.

h Yes, she gave me an invitation yesterday.

7 **Look at John's list and write sentences about what he has already done and what he hasn't done yet.**

1 He's already washed the car.

2 ....

3 ....

4 ....

5 ....

6 ....

7 ....

8 ....

*telephone bill – Telefonrechnung

8 Look at the picture and then decide if the sentences are True or False.

1 The red team have already scored four goals. ...True...
2 The first half hasn't finished yet. ....
3 The blue team haven't scored a goal yet. ....
4 The red number four has just got a red card. ....
5 The second half has already started. ....
6 The blue number ten hasn't taken the penalty yet. ....
7 It hasn't started raining yet. ....
8 A fan has just run onto the pitch. ....

9 Rewrite the sentences and include the word.

1 I've seen Janice. (just)
I've just seen Janice. ....
2 He's told me your secret. (already)
....
3 We haven't had lunch. (yet)
....
4 Paula's gone to the shops. (just)
....
5 The dog's had its puppies. (already)
....
6 Don hasn't bought a new car. (yet)
....
7 Mum's broken a cup. (just)
....
8 I haven't send him the email. (yet)
....

e-ZONE 10 Complete the postcard using the present perfect form of the verbs.

Hi Paula,
Week three of our European tour already. Time goes by too fast.
We [1]'ve already spent (already spend) time in France and Spain
and now we're in the UK. I'm in London! Can you believe it?
We've only been here two days but we [2]...................... (already have) a wonderful
time. We've done so many things. We [3]...................... (already be) on the London Eye
– fantastic and we [4]...................... (already see) Buckingham Palace but I
[5]...................... the Queen .... (not meet yet). Tomorrow we're going to do
some more sightseeing: the Tower of London, Hyde Park and Covent Garden. We
[6]...................... a show .... (not see yet) but mum [7]......................
(already promise) to take us to one tonight.
We've been so busy that we [8]...................... any shopping .... (not do yet) so I
[9]...................... you a present .... (not buy yet).
So far we've walked everywhere. We [10]...................... on the Underground
.... (not travel yet). London is so big. We [11]...................... (already get) lost
lots of times. But that's always fun. You find new exciting places.
More soon. Bye!

11 Put the words in order to make sentences.

1 shopping / We / yet / done / the / haven't

We haven't done the shopping yet.

2 bought / just / a / TV / We've / new

3 woken / yet / hasn't / She / up

4 sandwiches / You / two / already / had / have

5 games / They've / finished / just / computer / playing

6 baby / My / just / mum's / new / had / a

7 yet / I / Batman / seen / the / haven't / new / film

8 walk / I've / a / the / dog / taken / already / for

12 Make the positive sentences negative and the negative sentences positive.

1 I haven't tidied my room yet.

I've already tidied my room.

2 Oliver's already given me a present.

3 She hasn't phoned her mum yet.

4 Mum and dad have already gone out.

5 I've already done my exams.

6 They haven't had dinner yet.

7 Sally's already sold her skateboard.

8 We haven't found our dog yet.

13 Use the word prompts to write about you.

take / driving test — I've not taken my driving test yet. I'm too young!

decide / future job

fall off / bike

fly / airplane

go / abroad

break / leg

learn / swim

have / boy/girlfriend — that's none of your business!

And now go to the e-ZONE and do the Cartoon for Fun!

So (do/have) I / Neither (do/have) I

Hello! See me on the e·ZONE to discover more about *So (do/have) I / Neither (do/have) I* and to learn better when to use them.

Wenn du im Englischen „ich auch" oder „ich auch nicht" sagen möchtest, verwendest du **so** oder **neither** zusammen mit dem passenden Verb. Modale Hilfsverben (**can/can't**, **must/mustn't**, etc.) und **have** werden wiederholt – hier verwendest du kein **do/did**.

I **like** rap – **So do** I.	I **don't like** rock. – **Neither do** I.
I**'ve got** a laptop. – **So have** I.	I **haven't got** a laptop – **Neither have** I.
I **can play** the piano. – **So can** I.	I **can't play** the piano. – **Neither can** I.
I **went** to the cinema last night. – **So did** I.	I **didn't go** to the cinema last night. – **Neither did** I.

e·ZONE **1** **Underline the correct answers.**

1 **A** I want an ice cream.
B *So do I / Neither do I.*

2 **A** I live in Grange Road.
B *So do I / So have I.*

3 **A** I've got a test tomorrow.
B *So do I / So have I.*

4 **A** I've got a new bike.
B *So have I / Neither have I.*

5 **A** I don't like her.
B *So do I / Neither do I.*

6 **A** I don't eat meat.
B *Neither do I / Neither have I.*

7 **A** I haven't got any money.
B *So have I / Neither have I.*

8 **A** I haven't done my homework yet.
B *Neither do I / Neither have I.*

2 **Complete the dialogues with the sentences in the box.**

So do I. (2x)
Neither do I. (2x)
So have I. (2x)
~~Neither have I.~~ (2x)

1 **A** I haven't got a pet.
B Neither have I.

2 **A** I really like Brad Pitt.
B ....

3 **A** I've got a headache.
B ....

4 **A** I don't play tennis very well.
B ....

5 **A** I haven't seen this film.
B ....

6 **A** I don't get up early at the weekend.
B ....

7 **A** I've finished my homework.
B ....

8 **A** I go swimming three times a week.
B ....

3 **Match the sentences and replies.**

1 I collect postcards.
2 I don't walk to school.
3 I've lost my school bag.
4 I've not watched TV all day.
5 I can speak three languages.
6 I can't go to Dave's party.
7 I went to bed late last night.
8 I didn't enjoy the book.

a So have I.
b So can I.
c Neither can I.
d So did I.
e So do I.
f Neither have I.
g Neither did I.
h Neither do I.

e-ZONE **4** **Fill in the blanks and complete the dialogue. Choose from *So do/have I*, *Neither do/have I*.**

Lucy I love Beyoncé.
Emma 1 ......So do I.......... . She's brilliant.
Lucy I've got all her CDs.
Emma 2 .... All of them.
Lucy Actually I haven't got her first one.
Emma No, 3 ....
Lucy But I want to get it.
Emma 4 .... I'm going to get it tomorrow.
Lucy I don't think she's done a bad song.
Emma 5 .... They're all great.
Lucy I also think she's a great actress.
Emma 6 .... She's really great.
Lucy I've seen all her films.
Emma 7 .... I love them.
Lucy I've never seen her in a bad film.
Emma 8 .... She's always brilliant.
Lucy Actually I'm just joking. I think she's terrible really.
Emma Yeah 9 .... She's rubbish.

e-ZONE **5** **Complete with *so* or *neither*.**

1 **A** I only wear black clothes.
B .....So..... do I.

2 **A** I can stand on my head.
B .... can I.

3 **A** I bought a new T-shirt yesterday.
B .... did I.

4 **A** I don't want to go home yet.
B .... do I.

5 **A** I didn't watch all the film.
B .... did I.

6 **A** I haven't read this book yet.
B .... have I.

7 **A** I can't do this homework.
B .... can I.

8 **A** I've got a cold.
B .... have I.

6 **Write the replies.**

1 **A** I haven't been to London.
B Neither have I.

2 **A** I didn't go to school yesterday.
B ....

3 **A** I can't play tennis very well.
B ....

4 **A** I never read the newspaper.
B ....

5 **A** I saw a great film last night.
B ....

6 **A** I always have a drink of milk before I go to sleep.
B ....

7 **A** I've got two cats.
B ....

8 **A** I can see a problem with this.
B ....

And now go to the e-ZONE and do the Cartoon for Fun!

Present perfect + *ever* / *never*

Wenn du fragen möchtest, ob jemand irgendwann mal in der Vergangenheit etwas getan hat, verwendest du das *present perfect* mit dem Wort **ever**.

> Have you **ever** been to Hollywood?
> Has she **ever** met a famous person?

Wenn du sagen möchtest, dass jemand nie etwas getan hat, verwendest du das *present perfect* mit dem Wort **never**.

> I've **never** been to Hollywood.
> She's **never** met a famous person.

e·ZONE **1 Complete the poem with the words in the box.**

Have
phone
eaten
holidays
foreign
stay
ever
never
found
Paris
please
done

Too many questions

Have you ever [1]........................ foreign food?
Have you [2]........................ broken a bone?
Have you ever been to [3]........................?
[4]........................ you ever been to Rome?

No I've never eaten [5]........................ food.
And I've [6]........................ broken a bone.
And I never go on [7]........................ .
I prefer to [8]........................ at home.

Have you ever [9]........................ a wallet?
Have you ever lost your [10]........................?
No, I've never [11]........................ those things.
Now [12]........................ leave me alone.

2 Match questions and answers.

1 Have you ever been to a fancy dress party?
2 Have you ever had an accident?
3 Have you ever done a parachute jump?
4 Have you ever seen a ghost?
5 Have you ever broken your leg?
6 Have you ever got stuck in a lift?
7 Have you ever deleted an important computer file by mistake?
8 Have you ever written a short story?

a I've never seen one because they don't exist.
b Yes, I wore an Egyptian mummy costume.
c Yes, it was my dad's and he was furious with me.
d No, I haven't. I'm not very creative.
e No, I've never done one and I don't ever want to do one.
f No. I've never broken anything.
g I fell off my bike once but it wasn't very serious.
h Yes, I got stuck in one for half an hour. I was quite scared.

3 Put the words in order to make sentences or questions.

1 had / ever / you / dog / a / Have ....
2 accident / had / She's / an / never ....
3 been / never / They've / on / airplane / an ....
4 famous / she / person / ever / met / a / Has ....
5 dress / We've / fancy / been / to / never / a / party ....

e·ZONE **4** **Read the radio interview and complete it with the phrases in the box.**

- have you ever thought
- have you ever broken
- 've fallen into
- haven't broken
- 've been on TV
- 've broken
- 've written
- 've fallen out
- 've fallen off
- 've had
- 've crashed
- 've never thought
- 've met some famous people
- 've never broken

DJ In the studio today we have Arnold Bump. Arnold is the world's unluckiest man.

Arnold That's right. I hold the world record for the unluckiest man on Earth.

DJ So Arnold, how did you get that record?

Arnold It's quite simple. I [1]........................ a lot of accidents.

DJ Can you tell us about some?

Arnold Certainly. I [2]........................ the River Thames in London. I [3]........................ of a 20 m tree. I [4]........................ my bike about 20 times and I [5]........................ my car five times.

DJ Wow. And [6]........................ any bones?

Arnold I [7]........................ lots of bones. I think the only bone I [8]........................ is my left arm. No, I [9]........................ that one.

DJ It sounds terrible.

Arnold Well it's not all bad. I [10]........................ and I [11]........................ and I [12]........................ a book about it all.

DJ And [13]........................ about making a film about your life?

Arnold No, I [14]........................ about that but it's not a bad idea.

5 **Write the questions.**

1 *Have you ever fallen out of a tree*? (fall)
2 ....? (fall asleep)
3 ....? (be on TV)
4 ....? (win)
5 ....? (eat)
6 ....? (be)
7 ....? (travel by)
8 ....? (drive)

6 **Write your answers to the questions in 5.**

And now go to the e·ZONE and do the Cartoon for Fun!

will-future

Für Vorhersagen, spontane Entschlüsse oder Versprechen verwendest du die *will-future.*

I'll (= I **will**) **see** you tomorrow.	It **won't** (= It **will not**) **rain** tomorrow.
We'll come (= We **will come**) to see you.	He **won't** (= He **will not**) **know** the answer.
You'**ll** (= You **will**) **enjoy** it.	They **won't** (= They **will not**) **go** to Italy.

1 Write the short forms.

1 It will be sunny tomorrow.
It'll be sunny tomorrow.

2 I will not be late.
....

3 There will not be any fog.
....

4 My father will come and pick us up.
....

5 The rain will stop soon.
....

6 I will not come to your house tomorrow.
....

e-ZONE

2 Write the phrases in the correct places.

~~not come~~
not bite
like
be
rain
not sleep
not be
go

1 Don't invite Jim to your party – he hates parties, so he won't come .
2 There are some big clouds in the sky – I think it .... this afternoon.
3 Eat some more, or you .... hungry at 10 o'clock.
4 I don't feel very well. I think I .... to the doctor tomorrow.
5 My dog's really friendly – don't worry, he .... you!
6 I'm going to buy this CD for my mum's birthday – I'm sure she .... it!
7 You didn't do your homework?! Well, the teacher .... happy about that!
8 Don't drink coffee! It's 11 o'clock at night – you .... well.

3 Match the sentences from 2 with the pictures. Write 1–8 in the boxes.

4 **Write what the people think they *will* / *won't* do next weekend.**

1 Paul thinks he'll do his homework on Sunday.

2 Susan thinks .... Jenny on Friday night.

3 My dad thinks .... on Sunday morning.

4 My mum thinks .... on Saturday.

5 My brother thinks .... on Saturday morning.

6 I think .... on Sunday night!

e-ZONE **5** **Complete the text. Use *'ll* or *won't* and the verbs.**

What can I do on Saturday night? Well, perhaps I [1] 'll go (go) to Jane's party. Hmmm – but I [2]........................ (not know) anyone at her party, so it [3]........................ (not be) fun. OK – I [4]........................ (phone) Sam. I'm sure he [5]........................ (have) ideas about what we can do. Oh no! Sam's in London. OK – I [6]........................ (invite) Alison to the cinema. Oh – I forgot. We had an argument and we're not friends any more, so she certainly [7]........................ (not come).
OK – perhaps I [8]........................ (stay) at home and do my homework.
It [9]........................ (not kill) me!

6 **Complete the sentences. Use *'ll* or *won't* and a verb from the box.**

~~become~~
have
not have
be
get
take
live
send

When I leave school …

1 I 'll become a famous footballer.

2 I .... incredibly rich!

3 I .... in a really, really big house!

4 I .... married.

5 I .... six children.

6 I .... my family on holiday every year to Australia and the USA.

7 I .... all my children to university.

8 … and then: I .... any money any more!!

7 **Write six sentences about <u>you</u> when you leave school. What will/won't you do?**

And now go to the e-ZONE and do the Cartoon for Fun!

Appendix

TENSES (ZEITEN)

PRESENT TENSE

Present simple (Einfache Gegenwartsform)

Die Form des *Present simple* ist für alle Personen gleich.
Ausnahme: In der 3. Person Singular wird ein ***-s*** angehängt.

Positive Aussagen	Negative Ausagen	Fragen	Kurzantworten	
I **like** London.	I **don't (do not) like** London.	**Do/Don't** I **like** London?	Yes, I **do**.	No, I **don't**.
You **like** London.	You **don't (do not) like** London.	**Do/Don't** you **like** London?	Yes, you **do**.	No, you **don't**.
He **likes** London.	He **doesn't (does not) like** London.	**Does/Doesn't** he **like** London?	Yes, he **does**.	No, he **doesn't**.
She **likes** London.	She **doesn't (does not) like** London.	**Does/Doesn't** she **like** London?	Yes, she **does**.	No, she **doesn't**.
It **likes** fish.	It **doesn't (does not) like** fish.	**Does/Doesn't** it **like** fish?	Yes, it **does**.	No, it **doesn't**.
We **like** London.	We **don't (do not) like** London.	**Do/Don't** we **like** London?	Yes, we **do**.	No, we **don't**.
You **like** London.	You **don't (do not) like** London.	**Do/Don't** you **like** London?	Yes, you **do**.	No, you **don't**.
They **like** London.	They **don't (do not) like** London.	**Do/Don't** they **like** London?	Yes, they **do**.	No, they **don't**.

Present continuous / present progressive (Verlaufsform, *-ing*-Form)

Das *Present continuous* wird gebildet mit der richtigen Form von ***be*** und der ***-ing***-Form des Verbs.

Positive Aussagen	Negative Ausagen	Fragen	Kurzantworten	
I**'m** (**I am**) **playing** football.	I**'m not** (**I am not**) **playing** football.	**Am** I **playing** football?	Yes, I **am**.	No, **I'm not**.
You**'re** (**You are**) **playing** football.	You **aren't** (**You're not**) **playing** football.	**Are** you **playing** football?	Yes, you **are**.	No, you **aren't**./No, **you're not**.
He**'s** (**He is**) **playing** football.	He **isn't** (**He's not**) **playing** football.	**Is** he **playing** football?	Yes, he **is**.	No, he **isn't**./No, **he's not**.
She**'s** (**She is**) **playing** football.	She **isn't** (**She's not**) **playing** football.	**Is** she **playing** football?	Yes, she **is**.	No, she **isn't**./No, **she's not**.
It**'s** (**It is**) **raining**.	It **isn't** (**It's not**) **raining**.	**Is** it **raining**?	Yes it **is**.	No, it **isn't**./No, **it's not**.
We**'re** (**We are**) **playing** football.	We **aren't** (**We're not**) **playing** football.	**Are** we **playing** football?	Yes, we **are**.	No we **aren't**./No, we**'re not**.
You**'re** (**You are**) **playing** football.	You **aren't** (**You're not**) **playing** football.	**Are** you **playing** football?	Yes, you **are**.	No you **aren't**./No, you**'re not**.
They**'re** (**They are**) **playing** football.	They **aren't** (**They're not**) **playing** football.	**Are** they **playing** football?	Yes, they **are**.	No, they **aren't**./No, they**'re not**.

Present perfect – Regular verbs (Regelmäßige Verben)

Das *Present perfect* wird gebildet mit ***has*** / ***have*** und der dritten Form (*past participle* Form) des Verbs.

Positive Aussagen		Negative Aussage			Fragen			Kurzantworten	
I've (I have)	finished.	I	**haven't (have not)**	finished.	**Have**	I	finished?	Yes, I **have**.	No, I **haven't**.
You've (You have)		You				you		Yes, you **have**.	No, you **haven't**.
He's (He has)		He	**hasn't (has not)**		**Has**	he		Yes, he **has**.	No, he **hasn't**.
She's (She has)		She				she		Yes, she **has**.	No, she **hasn't**.
It's (It has)		It				it		Yes, it **has**.	No, it **hasn't**.
We've (We have)		We	**haven't (have not)**		**Have**	we		Yes, we **have**.	No, we **haven't**.
You've (You have)		You				you		Yes, you **have**.	No, you **haven't**.
They've (They have)		They				they		Yes, they **have**.	No, they **haven't**.

Present perfect + *already / yet*

Already stellst du zwischen ***have*** / ***has*** und das Verb, **yet** stellst du an das Satzende.

I'**ve already** washed the car.	I **haven't done** my homework **yet**.
We'**ve already** seen this film.	She **hasn't told** him **yet**.

Present perfect + *ever / never*

Ever und ***never*** stellst du zwischen ***have*** / ***has*** und die dritte Form des Verbs.

Have you **ever been** to Hollywood?	I'**ve never been** to Hollywood.
Has she **ever met** a famous person?	She'**s never met** a famous person.

PAST TENSE

Past simple – *was / were* (Einfache Vergangenheitsform)

Das *Past simple* wird bei regelmäßigen Verben mit ***-ed*** gebildet (siehe „regular verbs"), bei unregelmäßigen Verben mit der zweiten Form (siehe „irregular verbs").

Positive Aussage	Negative Aussage	Fragen	Kurzantworten	
I **was** tired.	I **wasn't (was not)** tired.	**Was/Wasn't** I tired?	Yes, I **was**.	No, I **wasn't (was not)**.
You **were** tired.	You **weren't (were not)** tired.	**Were/Weren't** you tired?	Yes, you **were**.	No, you **weren't (were not)**.
He **was** nice.	He **wasn't (was not)** nice.	**Was/Wasn't** he nice?	Yes, he **was**.	No, he **wasn't (was not)**.
She **was** nice.	She **wasn't (was not)** nice.	**Was/Wasn't** she nice?	Yes, she **was**.	No, she **wasn't (was not)**.
It **was** blue.	It **wasn't (was not)** blue.	**Was/Wasn't** it blue?	Yes, it **was**.	No, it **wasn't (was not)**.
We **were** busy.	We **weren't (were not)** busy.	**Were/Weren't** we busy?	Yes, we **were**.	No, we **weren't (were not)**.
You **were** busy.	You **weren't (were not)** busy.	**Were/Weren't** you busy?	Yes, you **were**.	No, you **weren't (were not)**.
They **were** busy.	They **weren't (were not)** busy.	**Were/Weren't** they busy?	Yes, they **were**.	No, they **weren't (were not)**.

Regular verbs (Regelmäßige Verben)

Positive Aussage	Negative Aussage
I lik**ed** London.	I **didn't (did not) like** London.
You laugh**ed** a lot.	You **didn't (did not) laugh** a lot.
He walk**ed** home.	He **didn't (did not) walk** home.
She look**ed** good.	She **didn't (did not) look** good.
It turn**ed** around.	It **didn't (did not) turn** around.
We cook**ed** dinner.	We **didn't (did not) cook** dinner.
You cook**ed** dinner.	You **didn't (did not) cook** dinner.
They lov**ed** the film.	They **didn't (did not) love** the film.

Irregular verbs (Unregelmäßige Verben)

Hier findest du eine Liste mit einer Auswahl der wichtigsten unregelmäßigen Verben.

Present	Past simple	Past participle	Übersetzung
be	was/were	been	*sein*
become	became	become	*werden*
begin	began	begun	*beginnen*
blow	blew	blown	*blasen*
break	broke	broken	*brechen*
bring	brought	brought	*bringen*
build	built	built	*bauen*
buy	bought	bought	*kaufen*
catch	caught	caught	*fangen*
choose	chose	chosen	*(aus)wählen*
come	came	come	*kommen*
cut	cut	cut	*schneiden*
dig	dug	dug	*graben*
do	did	done	*tun, machen*
draw	drew	drawn	*zeichnen*
dream	dreamt (dreamed)	dreamt (dreamed)	*träumen*
drink	drank	drunk	*trinken*
drive	drove	driven	*fahren, treiben*
eat	ate	eaten	*essen*
fall (asleep)	fell (asleep)	fallen (asleep)	*fallen; (einschlafen)*
feel	felt	felt	*fühlen*
fight	fought	fought	*kämpfen*
find	found	found	*finden*
fly	flew	flown	*fliegen*
forget	forgot	forgotten	*vergessen*
get	got	got	*bekommen, werden*
get up	got up	got up	*aufstehen*
give	gave	given	*geben*
go	went	gone	*gehen, fahren*
hang	hung	hung	*hängen*
have	had	had	*haben*
hear	heard	heard	*hören*
hide	hid	hidden	*(sich) verstecken*
hit	hit	hit	*schlagen*
hold	held	held	*(fest)halten*
hurt	hurt	hurt	*(sich) verletzen, schmerzen*
know	knew	known	*wissen, kennen*

Present	Past simple	Past participle	Übersetzung
lay	laid	laid	*legen*
learn	learnt (learned)	learnt (learned)	*lernen*
leave	left	left	*verlassen*
let	let	let	*lassen*
lie	lay	lain	*liegen*
lose	lost	lost	*verlieren*
make	made	made	*machen*
meet	met	met	*treffen*
put	put	put	*geben, setzen, stellen*
read	read	read	*lesen*
ride	rode	ridden	*reiten, fahren*
ring	rang	rung	*läuten*
run	ran	run	*laufen*
say	said	said	*sagen*
see	saw	seen	*sehen*
send	sent	sent	*senden, schicken*
shoot	shot	shot	*schießen*
show	showed	shown (showed)	*zeigen*
sing	sang	sung	*singen*
sink	sank (sunk)	sunk	*untergehen, sinken*
sit	sat	sat	*sitzen, sich setzen*
sleep	slept	slept	*schlafen*
smell	smelt (smelled)	smelt (smelled)	*riechen*
speak	spoke	spoken	*sprechen, sagen*
spend	spent	spent	*verbringen, ausgeben*
stand	stood	stood	*stehen*
steal	stole	stolen	*stehlen*
swim	swam	swum	*schwimmen*
take off	took off	taken off	*ausziehen*
take	took	taken	*nehmen*
teach	taught	taught	*lehren, unterrichten*
tell	told	told	*sagen, erzählen*
think	thought	thought	*denken*
wake (up)	woke (up)	woken (up)	*(auf)wachen*
win	won	won	*gewinnen*
write	wrote	written	*schreiben*

Past time expressions

Bei diesen Wörtern verwendest du beim Erzählen das *past*.

then	ago	later	after	one day	finally

FUTURE TENSE

going to-future (Zukunft mit *going to*)

Die *going-to-future* wird mit einer Form von **be** und **going to** und der Grundform des Vollverbs gebildet.

Positive Aussage		Negative Aussage		Fragen		Kurzantworten
I'm	**going to play** football.	I'**m not**	**going to play** football.	**Am** I	**going to play** football?	Yes, I **am**. / No **I'm not**.
You**'re**		You **aren't** (You**'re not**)		**Are** / **Aren't** you		Yes, you **are**. / No, you **aren't (you're not)**.
He**'s**		He **isn't** (He**'s not**)		**Is** / **Isn't** he		Yes, he **is**. / No, he **isn't (he's not)**.
She**'s**		She **isn't** (She**'s not**)		**Is** / **Isn't** she		Yes, she **is**. / No, she **isn't (she's not)**.
We**'re**		We **aren't** (We**'re not**)		**Are** / **Aren't** we		Yes, we **are**. / No, we **aren't (we're not)**.
You**'re**		You **aren't** (You**'re not**)		**Are** / **Aren't** you		Yes, you **are**. / No, you **aren't (you're not)**.
They**'re**		They **aren't** (They**'re not**)		**Are** / **Aren't** they		Yes, they **are**. / No, they **aren't (they're not)**.

will-future

Die *will-future* verwendest du, wenn du etwas vorhersagen möchtest oder versprichst.

Positive Aussagen	Negative Aussagen	Fragen	Kurzantworten	
I**'ll (I will)** see you tomorrow.	I **won't (will not)** see you tomorrow.	**Will** I see you tomorrow?	Yes, I **will**.	No, I **won't (will not)**.
You**'ll (You will)** see me tomorrow.	You **won't (will not)** see me tomorrow.	**Will** you see me tomorrow?	Yes, you **will**.	No, you **won't (will not)**.
He**'ll (He will)** her tomorrow.	He **won't (will not)** see her tomorrow.	**Will** he see her tomorrow?	Yes, he **will**.	No, he **won't (will not)**.
She**'ll (She will)** see him tomorrow.	She **won't (will not)** see him tomorrow.	**Will** she see him tomorrow?	Yes, she **will**.	No, she **won't (will not)**.
It**'ll (It will)** rain tomorrow.	It **won't (will not)** rain tomorrow.	**Will** it rain tomorrow?	Yes, it **will**.	No, it **won't (will not)**.
We**'ll (We will)** see you tomorrow.	We **won't (will not)** see you tomorrow.	**Will** we see you tomorrow?	Yes, we **will**.	No, we **won't (will not)**.
You**'ll (You will)** see me tomorrow.	You **won't (will not)** see me tomorrow.	**Will** you see me tomorrow?	Yes, you **will**.	No, you **won't (will not)**.
They**'ll (They will)** see you tomorrow.	They **won't (will not)** see you tomorrow.	**Will** they see you tomorrow?	Yes, they **will**.	No, they **won't (will not)**.

to be — affirmative, negative

Das Verb ***be*** wird wie das deutsche Verb **sein** verwendet.

Positive Aussage	Negative Aussage
I'**m** (**I am**) tired.	I'**m not** tired.
You'**re** (**You are**) clever.	You **aren't**/You'**re not** tired.
He'**s** (**He is**) nice.	He **isn't**/He'**s not** nice.
She'**s** (**She is**) in class 3B.	She **isn't**/She'**s not** in class 3B.
It'**s** (**It is**) blue.	It **isn't**/It'**s not** blue.
We'**re** (**We are**) busy.	We **aren't**/We'**re not** busy.
We'**re** (**We are**) busy.	We **aren't**/We'**re not** busy.
They'**re** (**They are**) twelve.	They **aren't**/They'**re not** twelve.

Questions with *be*

Fragen	Kurzantworten	
Am I tired?	Yes, I **am**.	No, I'**m not**.
Are/**Aren't** you tired?	Yes, you **are**.	No, you **aren't**./No, you'**re not**.
Is/**Isn't** he nice?	Yes, he **is**.	No, he **isn't**./No, he'**s not**.
Is/**Isn't** she in class 3B?	Yes, she **is**.	No, she **isn't**./No, she'**s not**.
Is/**Isn't** it blue?	Yes, it **is**.	No, it **isn't**./No, it'**s not**.
Are/**Aren't** we busy?	Yes, we **are**.	No, we **aren't**./No, we'**re not**.
Are/**Aren't** you busy?	Yes, you **are**.	No, you **aren't**./No, you'**re not**.
Are/**Aren't** they twelve?	Yes, they **are**.	No, they **aren't**./No, they'**re not**.

have got / haven't got

Have got wird wie das deutsche Verb **haben** (besitzen) verwendet.
Die richtige Form für die 3. Person der Gegenwart (**he**/**she**/**it**) ist ***has got***.

Positive Aussage	Negative Aussage	Fragen	Kurzantworten	
I'**ve got** (**I have got**) a dog.	I **haven't got** (**have not got**) a dog.	**Have**/**Haven't** I **got** a dog?	Yes, I **have**.	No, I **haven't**.
You'**ve got** (**You have got**) a dog.	You **haven't got** (**have not got**) a dog.	**Have**/**Haven't** you **got** a dog?	Yes, you **have**.	No, you **haven't**.
He'**s got** (**He has got**) a dog.	He **hasn't got** (**has not got**) a dog.	**Has**/**Hasn't** he **got** a dog?	Yes, he **has**.	No, he **hasn't**.
She'**s got** (**She has got**) a dog.	She **hasn't got** (**has not got**) a dog.	**Has**/**Hasn't** she **got** a dog?	Yes, she **has**.	No, she **hasn't**.
It'**s got** (**It has got**) big ears.	It **hasn't got** (**has not got**) big ears.	**Has**/**Hasn't** it **got** big ears?	Yes, it **has**.	No, it **hasn't**.
We'**ve got** (**We have got**) a dog.	We **haven't got** (**have not got**) a dog.	**Have**/**Haven't** we **got** a dog?	Yes, we **have**.	No, we **haven't**.
You'**ve got** (**You have got**) a dog.	You **haven't got** (**have not got**) a dog.	**Have**/**Haven't** you **got** a dog?	Yes, you **have**.	No, you **haven't**.
They'**ve got** (**They have got**) a dog.	They **haven't got** (**have not got**) a dog.	**Have**/**Haven't** they **got** a dog?	Yes, they **have**.	No, they **haven't**.

there is / there are

There is / ***there are*** wird verwendet, um auszudrücken, dass etwas vorhanden ist, oder dass es etwas gibt.

There's a monster in the tree. (= **There is** a monster in the tree.)

There are three frogs on the table.

Modal verbs (Modalverben)

Die wichtigsten Modalverben sind ***should*** / ***shouldn't***, ***have to*** / ***don't have to***, ***might*** / ***might not***, ***must*** / ***mustn't***, ***can*** / ***can't***, ***could*** / ***couldn't***, ***will*** / ***won't***, ***would*** / ***wouldn't***, ***shall*** / ***shall not***, and ***may*** / ***may not***.

I You He She It We You They	**can/can't** **must/mustn't** **should/shouldn't** **might/mightn't**	come today.	I You	**have to/don't have to**	go to school.
			He She It	**has to/doesn't have to**	
			We You They	**have to/don't have to**	

can / can't

Can ist ein Modalverb und wird deshalb immer in Verbindung mit einem Vollverb verwendet. Die Verneinung wird gebildet als ***cannot*** oder ***can't***.

Positive Aussagen	Negative Aussagen	Fragen	Kurzantworten	
I **can speak** French.	I **can't** (**cannot**) **speak** French.	**Can/Can't** I speak French?	Yes, I **can**.	No, I **can't**.
You **can speak** French.	You **can't** (**cannot**) **speak** French.	**Can/Can't** you speak French?	Yes, you **can**.	No, you **can't**.
He **can speak** French.	He **can't** (**cannot**) **speak** French.	**Can/Can't** he speak French?	Yes, he **can**.	No, he **can't**.
She **can speak** French.	She **can't** (**cannot**) **speak** French.	**Can/Can't** she speak French?	Yes, she **can**.	No, she **can't**.
It **can run** fast.	It **can't** (**cannot**) **run** fast.	**Can/Can't** it run fast?	Yes, it **can**.	No, it **can't**.
We **can speak** French.	We **can't** (**cannot**) **speak** French.	**Can/Can't** we speak French?	Yes, we **can**.	No, we **can't**.
You **can speak** French.	You **can't** (**cannot**) **speak** French.	**Can/Can't** you speak French?	Yes, you **can**.	No, you **can't**.
They **can speak** French.	They **can't** (**cannot**) **speak** French.	**Can/Can't** they speak French?	Yes, they **can**.	No, they **can't**.

like (doing)

Mit ***like doing*** sagst du, ob jemand gerne macht etwas oder sich gerne mit etwas beschäftigt. Gebildet wird es mit der einfachen Gegenwartsform von ***like*** + der ***-ing***-Form des folgenden Verbs.

Samantha **doesn't like reading** but she **likes listening** to music.	James **likes running** but he **doesn't like swimming**.

ADVERBS (ADVERBIEN)

Generell bildet man Adverbien, indem man an die Grundform des Adjektivs ***-ly*** anhängt.

usual – usual**ly**	sad – sad**ly**	furious – furious**ly**

Adverbs of manner (Adverbien der Art und Weise)

Mit Adverbien der Art und Weise beschreibst du, wie jemand etwas macht. Regelmäßige Adverbien werden mit ***-ly*** gebildet.

Regular (+ -ly) (Regelmäßig)		
bad – bad**ly**	quiet – quiet**ly**	happy – happi**ly**

Irregular (Unregelmäßig)	
fast – fast	good – well

Adverbs of frequency (always, often, usually, sometimes, never) (Häufigkeitsadverbien)

0%	→	→	→	100%
never	sometimes	often	usually	always

We **sometimes** go to the cinema on Fridays.
She's **always** happy.

IMPERATIVES (IMPERATIV / BEFEHLSFORMEN)

Die Befehlsform ist immer gleich wie die Grundform des Verbs (ohne ***to***). Die Verneinung wird mit ***do not*** (***don't***) + Grundform gebildet.

Run!	Don't run!
Sit down.	Don't sit down.
Open the window.	Don't open the window.

ARTICLES (ARTIKEL)

Indefinite article (Unbestimmter Artikel)

Der unbestimmte Artikel ***a*** wird vor einem zählbaren Hauptwort verwendet, ***an*** wird vor Selbstlauten verwendet.

a bike	**Vor den Vokalen (Selbstlauten): a, e, i, o, u**
a teacher	**an** egg /ən 'eg/
a dog	**an** apple /ən 'æpl/

Definite article (Bestimmter Artikel)

Der bestimmte Artikel, verwendet wie im Deutschen **der/die/das**, ist im Englischen immer ***the***.

the bike	**the** teacher	**the** dog

NOUNS (HAUPTWÖRTER)

Plural nouns – irregular plurals (Pluralformen)

Regelmäßige Pluralformen werden gebildet, indem ein ***-s*** angehängt wird.
Bei unregelmäßigen Formen wird am Wortende ***-y*** zu ***-ies*** (Vokal vor ***-y*** bleibt ***-y***) und ***-f*** oder ***-fe*** zu ***-ves***. Es gibt auch einige unregelmäßige Pluralformen.

Regelmäßig		
dog – dog**s**	snake – snake**s**	cat – cat**s**

Unregelmäßig					
baby – bab**ies**	leaf – lea**ves**	life – li**ves**	child – children	mouse – mice	foot – feet

PRONOUNS (PRONOMEN)

Question words (Fragewörter)

Who	**What**	**Where**	**How often**
Who is she?	**What**'s your name?	**Where** are you now?	**How often** do you go to the cinema?
Who are you?	**What** eats insects?	**Where** do you live?	
Who likes ice cream?	**What** does your dog eat?		
Who do you like?			

this / that, these / those

This / ***that***, ***these*** / ***those*** sind Demonstrativpronomen, die verwendet werden, um Nähe oder Ferne auszudrücken.
This / ***these*** beschreibt etwas in der Nähe, ***that*** / ***those*** etwas weiter Entferntes.

I like **this** jumper here.	I like **that** jumper over there.	I like **these** shoes here.	I like **those** shoes over there.

Possessives

Possessives stehen immer vor dem Hauptwort und zeigen an, wem oder zu wem etwas gehört.

I	you	he	she	it	we	they
my	**your**	**his**	**her**	**its**	**our**	**their**

Personal pronouns / Subject and object pronouns (Personalpronomen)

Personalpronomen können als Subjekt oder Objekt eines Satzes verwendet werden.
Das unpersönliche deutsche **man** kann im Englischen durch ***you***, ***they*** oder ***one*** ausgedrückt werden.

Subjekt	I	You	He	She	It	We	They
Objekt	me	you	him	her	it	us	them

one – ones

Wenn du ein Hauptwort nicht wiederholen willst, kannst du es durch ***one*** / ***ones*** ersetzen.

What **book** are you reading? **One** about a man travelling around Africa.
What **kind of books** do you like? **Ones** about travel.

some – any

Wenn du etwas Unzählbares beschreibst, verwendest du ***some***.
Wenn du fragen willst, ob es etwas gibt, oder wenn du sagen willst, dass es etwas nicht gibt, verwendest du ***any***.

some	**any**	
We've got **some** cheese.	We haven't got **any** cheese.	Is there **any** milk in the fridge?
I've got **some** money.	I haven't got **any** money.	Have we got **any** strawberries?
Would you like **some** soup?	There aren't **any** onions in the kitchen.	Do you want **any** chocolate?

whose + possessive *'s* (Genitiv)

Wenn du fragen willst, wem etwas gehört, verwendest du ***whose***. Wenn du mit einem Namen antwortest, fügst du das Possessiv ***'s*** an.

Whose is this book?	It's Amanda**'s** (book).
Whose book is this?	It's Harry Potter**'s** (book).

Possessive pronouns (Possessivpronomen)

Besitzanzeigende Fürwörter zeigen an, wem etwas gehört.

It's **my** book. It's **mine**.	It's **his** book. It's **his**.	It's **our** book. It's **ours**.
It's **your** book. It's **yours**.	It's **her** book. It's **hers**.	It's **their** book. It's **theirs**.

PREPOSITIONS (PRÄPOSITIONEN)

Präpositionen stehen vor einem Hauptwort oder Pronomen und zeigen die Richtung, den Ort, oder die Zeit (siehe „time prepositions") an.

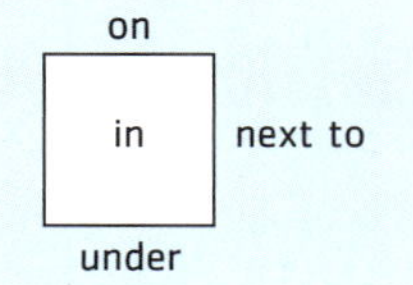

Time prepositions (*in, on, at*) (Präpositionen der Zeit)

My birthday is **on** February 12th / May 28th / September 5th.
My sister's birthday is **in** December / April / June.
The film starts **at** 7 o'clock / half past eight / six forty-five.

We have Maths **in** the morning / in the afternoon.
We go to bed late **at** night.

Prepositions of place (Directions) (Präpositionen des Ortes)

at	by	behind	in	in front of	inside	near
next to	on	opposite	outside	over	round	under

ADJECTIVES (ADJEKTIVE)

as … as

Wenn du sagen willst, dass etwas (nicht) gleich ist wie etwas anderes, verwendest du ***(not) as … as***.

I am **as** intelligent **as** my sister.

Comparatives & Superlatives (Vergleiche & Steigerung der Adjektive)

Einsilbige Adjektive steigerst du mit ***-er*** und ***-est***. Bei mehr als zwei Silben steigerst du mit ***more*** und ***most***.
Eine Auflistung der am häufigsten verwendeten Adjektivsteigerungen findest du hier.

My bike is bigg**er** than your bike.

My mum is **the most intelligent** person in our family.

Adjective	Comparative	Superlative
bad	worse	worst
big	bigg**er**	bigg**est**
cold	cold**er**	cold**est**
easy	easi**er**	easi**est**
fast	fast**er**	fast**est**
good	bett**er**	**best**
hot	hott**er**	hott**est**
long	long**er**	long**est**
new	new**er**	new**est**
old	old**er**	old**est**
rich	rich**er**	rich**est**
safe	safe**r**	safe**st**
small	small**er**	small**est**
strong	strong**er**	strong**est**
tall	tall**er**	tall**est**
young	young**er**	young**est**

Adjective	Comparative	Superlative
funny	funni**er**	funni**est**
happy	happi**er**	happi**est**
heavy	heavi**er**	heavi**est**
pretty	pretti**er**	pretti**est**
ugly	ugli**er**	ugli**est**
beautiful	**more** beautiful	**most** beautiful
boring	**more** boring	**most** boring
dangerous	**more** dangerous	**most** dangerous
difficult	**more** difficult	**most** difficult
exciting	**more** exciting	**most** exciting
expensive	**more** expensive	**most** expensive
handsome	**more** handsome	**most** handsome
important	**more** important	**most** important
intelligent	**more** intelligent	**most** intelligent
poisonous	**more** poisonous	**most** poisonous
popular	**more** popular	**most** popular
relaxing	**more** relaxing	**most** relaxing

CONJUNCTIONS (KONJUNKTIONEN)

Linking words (*and*, *but*, *because*)

Konjunktionen verbinden Hauptsätze und Nebensätze miteinander.

We went to the cinema **and** watched a great film.
but it was closed.
because we had free tickets.

So (do/have) I / Neither (do/have) I

Wenn du jemandem zustimmen willst („ich auch"), verwendest du ***So do I***. Bei einer negativen Aussage, der du zustimmst („ich auch nicht"), verwendest du ***Neither do I***.
Bei Modalverben und ***have*** wiederholst du das Verb, ansonsten verwendest du ***do***.

I **like** rap. – **So do I.**	I **don't like** rock. – **Neither do I.**
I**'ve got** a laptop. – **So have I.**	I **haven't got** a laptop. – **Neither have I.**
I **can** play the piano. – **So can I.**	I **can't play** the piano. – **Neither can I.**
I **went** to the cinema last night. – **So did I.**	I **didn't go** to the cinema last night. – **Neither did I.**

why / because

Um die Ursache von etwas zu erfragen bzw. zu begründen verwendest du ***why*** bzw. ***because***.

Why did you go to the store? – **Because** I needed bread.

QUANTITY / MEASUREMENT (MENGENANGABEN)

How much is/are...?

Mit ***how much*** wird nach der Menge (bei nichtzählbaren Hauptwörtern) oder nach dem Preis gefragt.

How much ice cream do you eat every day?	**How much** is the ice cream?	**How much** money have you got?	**How much** are the trainers?

Ordinal numbers

Cardinal	Ordinal
1 one	**first**
2 two	**second**
3 three	**third**
4 four	four**th**
5 five	fif**th**
6 six	six**th**
7 seven	seven**th**
8 eight	eigh**th**
9 nine	nin**th**
10 ten	ten**th**
11 eleven	eleven**th**
12 twelve	twelf**th**
13 thirteen	thirteen**th**
14 fourteen	fourteen**th**
15 fifteen	fifteen**th**

Cardinal	Ordinal
16 sixteen	sixteen**th**
17 seventeen	seventeen**th**
18 eighteen	eighteen**th**
19 nineteen	nineteen**th**
20 twenty	twentie**th**
21 twenty-one	twenty-**first**
30 thirty	thirtie**th**
40 forty	fortie**th**
50 fifty	fiftie**th**
60 sixty	sixtie**th**
70 seventy	seventie**th**
80 eighty	eightie**th**
90 ninety	ninetie**th**
100 hundred	hundred**th**
101 a/one hundred and one	**the (one) hundred and first**

Wordlist

A

activity	Aktivität
actually	eigentlich; tatsächlich
I'm afraid (so)/(not)	leider/leider nicht
against	gegen
age	Alter
(two days) ago	vor (zwei Tagen)
air	Luft
alarm	Angst; hier: Alarm
all day	den ganzen Tag
all the time	die ganze Zeit
almost	fast, beinahe
already	schon
amazing	erstaunlich
an	ein e, r, s
another	noch eine(r, s); ein andere(r, s)
any	irgendein/e
(not) any longer	nicht mehr
(not) any more	nicht mehr
anybody	jeder; ein jeder
anywhere	überall(hin); irgendwo(hin)
area	Gebiet, Region
argument	Wortwechsel; Streit
art	Kunst
as … as …	(genau)so … wie …
as well	auch, ebenfalls
(not) at all	gar nicht
aunt	Tante
awesome	beeindruckend

B

back	Rücken
bacon	Speck
bank	Bank; Ufer
bark	bellen
base	Fuß, Basis
bat	Schläger
bath	Bad
battle	Kampf, Schlacht
beach	Strand
bear	Bär
beat	schlagen
become	werden
behind	hinter
believe	glauben
bell	Glocke; Klingel
below	unten; unterhalb
belt	Gürtel
beside	neben
between	zwischen
bike	Fahrrad
bird	Vogel
bite	Biss; beißen
blonde	blond
blood	Blut
blouse	Bluse
body	Körper
(be) born	geboren
borrow (from)	ausleihen (von)
both	beide
bottle	Flasche
bottom	unten
bowl	Schüssel
break	Pause
bright	hell, leuchtend
Britain	Großbritannien
British	britische (r, s)
build	bauen
bump into …	mit … zusammenstoßen
busy	beschäftigt
buy	kaufen
by	bei, mit
bye	tschüss

C

cage	Käfig
camera	Kamera, Fotoapparat
camp	Zeltlager
candle	Kerze
care about …	sich aus … etw. machen
care for	sich kümmern um
careful	vorsichtig
carry	tragen; hier: übertragen
centre	Zentrum, Mitte
certainly	sicher(lich); bestimmt
change	(sich) (ver)ändern
check out	überprüfen
chemist's	Apotheke, Drogerie
child, children	Kind, Kinder
choose	auswählen
church	Kirche
classmate	Klassenkamerad/in, Mitschüler/in
clean	sauber; sauber machen, reinigen, putzen
climb	(hinauf)steigen; klettern
clothes (no pl)	Kleider, Kleidung
cloud	Wolke
clue	Hinweis, Anhaltspunkt; Tipp
coat	Mantel
coffee	Kaffee
coin	Münze, Geldstück
collect	sammeln
comfortable	bequem
compare	vergleichen
concentrate	(sich) konzentrieren
connect	anschließen; verbinden
continue	andauern; weitergehen
cook	Koch/Köchin; kochen
could	könnte(n)
count	zählen
cover	bedecken
crash	zu Bruch fahren
create	erschaffen, kreieren
cross	durchqueren, überqueren; Kreuz
cry	Schrei; weinen; schreien
cup	Tasse
cupboard	Schrank
curtain	Vorhang
cut	schneiden
cycle	Rad fahren

D

dancer	Tänzer/in
danger	Gefahr
dangerous	gefährlich
dark	Dunkelheit; dunkel
daughter	Tochter
dead	tot
deep	tief
definitely	eindeutig, definitiv; auf jeden Fall
delete	streichen, löschen
desert	Wüste
desk	Schreibtisch
dessert	Nachtisch, Dessert
diary	Tagebuch
dictionary	Wörterbuch
die	sterben
different	anders, andere (r, s); verschieden
difficult	schwierig, schwer
dig	graben
directions	Anweisungen
dirty	dreckig, schmutzig
disappointed	enttäuscht
discover	herausfinden, entdecken
the dishes (pl)	das Geschirr
doctor	Arzt/Ärztin
dolphin	Delphin
done	fertig
doom	Verhängnis
double	doppelt, Doppel-
down	hinunter, hinab
draw	malen; zeichnen
dream	Traum; träumen
dress	Kleid
driving test	Fahrprüfung
drop	fallen lassen
drums	Schlagzeug
dry	trocknen; trocken

E

each other	einander, gegenseitig
early	früh
earth	Erde
east	östlich, Ost-; Osten
something else	noch etwas
empty	leer
ending	Ende, Schluss
enjoy	genießen
enough	genügend, ausreichend, genug
especially	besonders
even	sogar, nicht mal
ever	je
every	jede(r, s)
everybody	jede(r); alle
everyone	jede(r); alle
everything	alles
everywhere	überall
for example	zum Beispiel
excited	aufgeregt
exciting	aufregend; spannend

exotic exotisch; fremdländisch
explain erklären
extra mehr; besonders; Extra

F

fall over hinfallen; umfallen
famous berühmt
farmer Bauer/Bäuerin, Farmer/in
fat Fett; fett
fault Schuld
favourite Lieblings-
few ein paar; einige
fight kämpfen
fill in eintragen
final Finale
finally schließlich; endlich
find out herausfinden
finish beenden; vervollständigen
flight Fliegen; Flug
floor Boden; Stockwerk
flower Blume
follow folgen
be fond (of) (etw.) gerne mögen
fool Narr
forest Wald
forgetful vergesslich
fork Gabel
free befreien; frei, kostenlos
freeze gefrieren; einfrieren
fridge Kühlschrank
friendly freundlich
front Vorderseite
in front (of) vor
front door Vordertür; Haustür
funny lustig, komisch
furious wütend
future zukünftig

G

gate Tor
genius Genie
gentleman (pl gentlemen) Gentleman; Herr
geography Erdkunde, Geografie
get erhalten, bekommen; holen
get married heiraten
get out (of) hinauskommen/herauskommen (aus)
get up aufstehen
ghost Geist
girlfriend Freundin
give up aufgeben
glad froh
go on weitergehen; -machen
go to sleep einschlafen
goal Tor
goat Ziege
god Gott
good-looking gutaussehend
goose (pl geese) Gans
grandchild (pl -children) Enkelkind
granddad Großvater
grandparents (pl) Großeltern
grape Traube
ground (Erd)boden, Erde
group Gruppe
grow wachsen; hier: werden
grow up aufwachsen
guess (er)raten
guest Gast
gun Schusswaffe
guy Kerl, Typ
guys (informal) Leute
gymnastics (pl) Turnen

H

hairy haarig, stark behaart
ham Schinken
happen geschehen
hard hart
haunted Spuk-
Have fun! Viel Spaß!
headache Kopfschmerzen
healthy gesund
hear hören
heat Wärme; Hitze
heaven Himmel
heavy schwer
height Höhe
Here you are. Hier, bitte!, Bitte schön!
hers ihre(r, s)
high hoch
hill Hügel; Anhöhe
history Geschichte
hold (fest)halten
hole Loch
hopefully hoffnungsvoll; hoffentlich
horse Pferd
how to wie man
hug umarmen
huge riesig, riesengroß
human Mensch; menschlich
hunt jagen; jagd
hurt wehtun, schmerzen;
husband Ehemann

I

ice Eis
ice skating Schlittschuh laufen
I'd like ich möchte
if wenn
ill krank
illness Krankheit
imagine sich vorstellen
important wichtig
ink Tinte
interested (in) interessiert (an)
interesting interessant
into in
invite einladen

J

jam Marmelade
jewel Juwel
jewellery Schmuck
join (in) teilnehmen (an), mitmachen (bei)
joke Witz
journey Reise
jungle Dschungel
junk food Schnellgerichte; ungesundes Essen
Just kidding! War nur ein Scherz.

K

kick Tritt, Stoß; treten, kicken
what kind (of) was für
kiss küssen
kitchen Küche
knife (pl knives) Messer
knock Klopfen; klopfen
know wissen; kennen

L

lake See
lamp Lampe
land Land; landen
language Sprache
large groß
late (zu) spät
later später
laugh lachen
laughter Gelächter
lazy faul; träge
leaf (pl leaves) Blatt
at least mindestens, wenigstens
leave verlassen, weggehen
lemon Zitrone
less (than) weniger (als)
let go loslassen
Let's see. Schauen wir mal.
library Bibliothek, Bücherei
lie liegen; sich legen
life (pl lives) Leben
light leicht; Licht
list Liste
a little ein bisschen
lock abschließen
look Blick, Aussehen
look after sich kümmern um
look at betrachten, sehen
look for suchen nach
lose verlieren
be lost sich verirrt haben
a lot (of) viel(e)
lots of viel, jede Menge
low niedrig, schwach
be lucky Glück haben

M

mad wahnsinnig; böse
made of aus … gemacht
magic Magie, Zauber
(shopping) mall (große) Einkaufspassage
man (pl men) Mann
many viele
map (Land)karte
mask Maske
match zuordnen
It doesn't matter. Das ist nicht wichtig.
maybe vielleicht
mean gemein
mean bedeuten; meinen
meat Fleisch
medal Medaille
medicine (no pl) Medizin, Medikament(e)
memory Gedächtnis
menu Speisekarte
mess Unordnung, Durcheinander
messy unordentlich, schlampig
middle Mitte
might könnte; vielleicht (tun, sein)
mild sanft; mild
mile Meile
million Million

mine	meine(r, s)
mineral water	Mineralwasser
miss	vermissen, verpassen
mobile (phone)	Handy
mode	Modus
moon	Mond
most	am meisten; die meisten
mountain	Berg
mouse (pl mice)	Maus
move	(sich) bewegen; umziehen
mushroom	Pilz
musician	Musiker/in

N

nail	Nagel
naked	nackt, unbekleidet
neck	Hals; Nacken
need	brauchen
neighbour	Nachbar/in
Neither do I.	Ich auch nicht.
nervous	nervös
never	nie(mals)
news (pl)	Nachrichten
newsagent's	Zeitungsgeschäft
newspaper	Zeitung
no longer	nicht mehr
no one	niemand
nobody	niemand
noise	Lärm, Krach; Geräusch
none	keine(r, s)
north	nördlich, Nord-; Norden
note	Notiz
nothing	nichts

O

object	Objekt, Gegenstand, Sache
ocean	Meer, Ozean
of course	natürlich
off	aus; weg
office	Büro
officer	Offizier/in; Beamtin/ Beamter
on my own	alleine
once	einmal
onto	auf
opposite	gegenüber
order	bestellen; Reihenfolge
other	andere, r, s
ours	unsere(r, s)
outdoor	im Freien
out of	aus
outer space	Weltraum, Weltall
outside	außen, außerhalb
over	über, herüber
owl	Eule
own	eigene(r, s)
owner	Besitzer/in, Eigentümer/in

P

pack	packen
pain	Schmerz
paint	malen, streichen
painting	Bild, Gemälde
pair	Paar
paragraph	Absatz, Abschnitt
part	Teil
partner	Partner/in
pass (a test)	(eine Prüfung) bestehen
past	nach; vorbei an
path	Weg, Pfad
pay	bezahlen
pea	Erbse
peace	Friede
peach	Pfirsich
pear	Birne
people (pl)	Leute, Menschen
perhaps	vielleicht
person	Person, Mensch
photo	Foto
photograph	Foto(grafie)
physical education (PE)	Sport(unterricht)
pick up	aufheben, abholen
pie	Pastete
piece	Stück
pig	Schwein
pill	Tablette
plan	plane
plan (house)	Lageplan
plane	Flugzeug
plant	Pflanze
play	Theaterstück; Spiel
pocket	(Hosen-)Tasche
pocket money	Taschengeld
point (at)	zeigen (auf)
poison	Gift
poisonous	giftig
police	Polizei
popular	beliebt
possible	möglich
post	Post
post office	Postamt
pot	Topf
power	Kraft
powerful	mächtig
practice	Übung
practise	üben; Übung
present	Geschenk
pretty	hübsch
price	Preis
private	privat, Privat-
probably	wahrscheinlich
promise	versprechen; Versprechen
proud	stolz
pull	ziehen
pumpkin	Kürbis
purple	violett, lila
push	schieben, drücken
put	setzen, legen, stellen
put on	anziehen

Q

quarter	Viertel(stunde)
queen	Königin
quiet	leise, ruhig
quite	ziemlich

R

race	rennen, rasen; Rennen
rain	Regen; regnen
rainfall	Niederschlag
rainy	regnerisch
react	reagieren
ready	fertig, bereit
reason	Grund
record	Rekord
record	aufzeichnen
repeat	wiederholen
report	Bericht
rescue	Rettung; retten
rest	Rest; Ruhe
rhyme	Reim
rich	reich
Right here.	Hab' ich hier.
right now	jetzt gerade
round	um ... herum; rund
rub	reiben
rubbish	Müll
rug	Teppich
rule	Regel; beherrschen

S

safe	sicher
sail	Segeln
salad	Salat
salt	Salz
the same	der-/die-/dasselbe
save	retten
scare	Angst machen, erschrecken
be scared	Angst haben
scary	furchterregend; unheimlich
science	Naturwissenschaft
scientist	Wissenschaftler/in
score	erreichen, erzielen (Tore); Punktestand, Spielstand
scream	schreien; kreischen
screen	Leinwand; Bildschirm
sea	Meer
seat	(Sitz)platz
second	Sekunde
secret	geheim; Geheimnis
sell	verkaufen
series	Serie; Reihe
serious	ernst
several	einige, mehrere
shape	Form
share	teilen
sheep (pl sheep)	Schaf
shine	scheinen
shocked	schockiert, entsetzt
shopping centre	Einkaufszentrum
should	sollte
shower	Regenschauer
shut	schließen, zumachen
sick	krank
feel sick	sich schlecht fühlen
side	Seite
sign	Zeichen, Schild
simple	einfach
situation	Situation, Lage
size	Größe
skate	Rollschuh fahren
sky	Himmel
sleep	Schlaf
slice	Scheibe
smart	schlau
smell	riechen
smile	Lächeln
snack	Snack, Imbiss
sneeze	niesen
sniff	riechen, schnuppern
snow	Schnee

so-called	sogenannt
somebody	jemand
someone	jemand
something	etwas
sometimes	manchmal
somewhere	irgendwo
son	Sohn
soon	bald
sort	Sorte, Art
south	südlich, Süd-; Süden
southern	südlich, Süd-
space	Weltall
speech bubble	Sprechblase
speed	Geschwindigkeit, Tempo
spend	ausgeben (Geld); verbringen (Zeit)
spill	verschütten
square	Quadrat, Platz
stage	Bühne
stain	Fleck
stand up (for)	sich einsetzen (für)
starter	Vorspeise
station	Bahnhof; Station
statue	Statue, Standbild
stay (at)	übernachten (bei)
stay up late	lang aufbleiben
steal	stehlen
step	Stufe
stick	Stock; kleben
still	(immer) noch, noch immer
stomach	Magen
straight ahead	genau vor, geradeaus
straight on	geradeaus
straightaway	sofort
strange	sonderbar
stranger	Fremde/r
strawberry	Erdbeere
strong	stark
strongest	stärkste(r, s)
student	Student/in, Studierende/r; Schüler/in
study	studieren; lernen
stuff (informal)	Zeug
stupid	dumm, blöd
subject (school)	(Schul)fach
such	solche, r, s
suddenly	plötzlich, auf einmal
suggestion	Vorschlag
summary	Zusammenfassung
sun	Sonne
supermarket	Supermarkt
surf (the net)	surfen (im Internet)
swimmer	Schwimmer/in
switch off	abschalten

T

take off	abnehmen; abheben, starten
take out	herausnehmen
tale	Geschichte
tan	(Sonnen)bräune
task	Aufgabe
teach	unterrichten
teapot	Teekanne
tear	Träne
television	Fernsehgerät
temperature	Temperatur
term	Semester; Schuljahresabschnitt
terror	schreckliche Angst
text message	SMS
(more) than	(mehr) als
thank God	Gott sei Dank
their	ihr(e)
theirs	ihr(e, es)
them	sie, ihnen
these	diese
thick	dick
thief (pl thieves)	Dieb/in
thirsty	durstig
throat	Hals
through	durch
throw	werfen
thunderstorm	Gewitter
tidy	aufräumen
tight	fest
till	bis
today	heute
toe	Zeh(e)
together	zusammen, gemeinsam
toilet	Toilette, Klo
tomorrow	morgen
tongue	Zunge
tonight	heute Abend
too	zu; auch
tooth (pl teeth)	Zahn
total	gesamt; völlig
touch	berühren
tourist	Tourist/in
towards	in Richtung, auf ... zu
towel	Handtuch
toy	Spielzeug
train	trainieren
train	Zug
trainer	Turnschuh; Trainer/in
travel	reisen
trip	Ausflug, Reise
get into trouble	Ärger bekommen
try	versuchen
turn off	abschalten
turn on	einschalten
twin	Zwilling, Zwillings-
type (of)	Art; Typ; Sorte
tyre	Reifen

U

ugly	hässlich
uncle	Onkel
underline	unterstreichen
unfortunately	unglücklicherweise
unfriendly	unfreundlich
uniform	Uniform
university	Universität
until	bis
unusual	ungewöhnlich
upon	auf, an
upstairs	oben
up to	bis zu
usually	gewöhnlich, normalerweise

V

valley	Tal
vegetable	Gemüse
vet	Tierarzt, Tierärztin
village	Dorf
voice	Stimme
volume	Volumen; Lautstärke

W

waiter/waitress	Bedienung, Kellner/in
wall	Wand
wallet	Brieftasche
war	Krieg
wardrobe	Kleiderschrank
washing	Wäsche
do the washing-up	abspülen
waste of time	Zeitverschwendung
watch	beobachten; zuschauen
watch out	aufpassen; Achtung!
watch TV	fernsehen
waterfall	Wasserfall
wave	winken
wear	tragen
weather	Wetter
weigh	wiegen
weird	merkwürdig, seltsam, komisch
wet	nass
whale	Wal
What about ...	Was ist mit ...?
What for?	Warum?, Wofür?
What's going on?	Was ist los?
What's the matter?	Was ist los?
What's up?	Was ist los?
wherever	wo(hin) auch immer
which	welche(r, s)
while	während
whole	ganz
whose	wessen
wide	weit
wife (pl wives)	Ehefrau
will	werden
windy	windig
wing	Flügel
wipe	abwischen, abputzen
witch	Hexe
without	ohne
wolf (pl wolves)	Wolf
woman (pl women)	Frau
(no) wonder	(kein) Wunder
wood	Wald, Holz
wool	Wolle
work	arbeiten; funktionieren; Arbeit
work out	ausrechnen; hier: trainieren
worker	Arbeiter/in
be worried	sich Sorgen machen
be worth	wert sein

Y

not yet	noch nicht
yours	deine (r, s), Ihre (r, s)
youth	Jugend

Key

Present simple

1
2 watches
3 plays
4 is
5 eats
6 goes
7 talks
8 washes
9 leaves
10 buys
11 switches
12 has

2
2 doesn't watch the news.
3 doesn't play football.
4 don't study French.
5 don't listen to hip-hop.
6 don't eat ham.
7 don't like her sister.
8 doesn't read novels.

3
2 He doesn't live in London.
3 You don't know Peter.
4 They don't play volleyball every Sunday.
5 Liam doesn't like Jessica.
6 She doesn't want to be a pilot.
7 Jenny and Rob aren't teachers.
8 We don't run 5 km every day.

4
2 is
3 are
4 likes
5 like
6 wants
7 leaves
8 want
9 enjoys
10 don't like
11 spend
12 doesn't listen
13 wears
14 don't like
15 is
16 hates
17 are
18 are
19 like
20 is
21 like
22 doesn't know
23 am not

5
2 What are his / Paul's favourite subjects?
3 What does he / Paul want to be?
4 Does he / Oliver like sport?
5 What does he / Oliver buy?
6 What's his / Oliver's favourite colour?
7 How old are Oliver and Paul?
8 Does Paul know Oliver likes his girlfriend?

8
On Tuesdays I *play the guitar but I don't play the drums.*
On Wednesdays I *study/do my homework but I don't watch TV.*
On Thursdays I *go roller-skating but I don't play video games.*
On Fridays I *go to the cinema but I don't go dancing.*
On Saturdays I *get up at 11:00 but I don't get up at 9:00.*
On Sundays I *ride a/my bicycle but I don't wash it.*

Past simple – revision

1
2 give – gave
3 fall – fell
4 find – found
5 break – broke
6 hit – hit
7 sit – sat
8 meet – met
9 run – ran
10 hold – held

2
4, 5, 7, 8

3
1 played
2 held
3 drove
4 ate
5 swam
6 went
7 met
8 kissed
9 flew
10 had

4
2 ate
3 watched
4 went
5 met
6 gave
7 walked
8 dreamed / dreamt

Past simple – negation

1
a 3 b 6 c 1 d 8
e 5 f 7 g 2 h 4

2
2 asked
3 saw
4 went
5 didn't ask
6 didn't work
7 didn't go
8 didn't see

Past simple – questions

1
2 Did you go with your brother and sister?
3 Did you stay in a hotel?
4 Did you cook your own food?
Order of answers: 4, 1, 2, 3

2
1 **B** didn't see
2 **A** Did – do; **B** didn't do
3 **A** Did – go; **B** went
4 **A** Did – watch; **B** didn't watch

3
2 Did you see your friends last Saturday?
3 Did the teacher give you homework last night?
4 Did your parents go out last weekend?

Past simple – negation and questions

1
5, 7, 3, 1, 11, 9, 2, 6, 8, 10, 4

2
2 c 3 c 4 a

3
2 went
3 didn't come
4 was
5 wasn't
6 didn't like
7 didn't pay
8 didn't have
9 did you go
10 wasn't
11 didn't eat
12 didn't have
13 did you talk
14 didn't talk
15 didn't want
16 wasn't

Irregular verbs

1
2 broke
3 found
4 gave
5 got
6 had
7 caught
8 said
9 read
10 took

2
2 read 3 said 4 got
5 had 6 found 7 caught
8 took 9 gave 10 broke

3
2 took
3 said
4 went
5 watched
6 waited
7 was
8 phoned
9 didn't have
10 started
11 started
12 got
13 stopped
14 looked
15 found
16 was
17 picked
18 ran
19 caught

one – ones

1
1 e 2 b 3 h 4 g
5 d 6 c 7 a 8 f

2
1 One 2 ones 3 one
4 one 5 one 6 ones

3
2 ones 3 ones 4 one
5 one 6 one 7 one
8 one 9 one 10 ones
11 ones 12 ones

why / because

1
1 h 2 g 3 a 4 b 5 e
6 i 7 d 8 f 9 c

2
1 **B** Because
2 **B** Why
A Because
3 **A** because
B Why
A Because
4 **A** Why
B Because
5 **B** Why
A Because
6 **A** because
B Why
A Because

3
2 Why did Jamie jump (out of bed)?
3 Why was the house (empty)?
4 Why didn't Jamie / did Jamie not have (breakfast)?
6 Why did Jamie shout ('Oh no!')?

should / shouldn't

1 **2** e **3** a **4** g **5** i **6** h
7 c **8** b **9** d

2
2 you should go to bed early
3 shouldn't call him bad names
4 shouldn't worry so much
5 should charge it more often
6 should have a party
7 shouldn't stay out late

3
2 You should say you're sorry.
3 We shouldn't make any noise.
4 We should take the dog for a walk this afternoon.
5 I shouldn't eat so much chocolate.
6 We should invite him to the cinema.

4 **b** 6 **c** 1 **d** 2 **e** 4 **f** 3

Comparatives

1 **2** b **3** b **4** b **5** a **6** a **7** a **8** a

2
2 older
3 better
4 more dangerous
5 safe
6 colder
7 intelligent
8 ugly

3
2 faster
3 more popular
4 more expensive
5 more intelligent
6 prettier
7 bigger
8 more poisonous

4
1 older
2 taller
3 more intelligent
4 more handsome
5 more friendly
6 richer
7 better
8 stronger
9 faster
10 happier

as … as

1 **2** T **3** F **4** T **5** F
6 T **7** F **8** F

2
2 The Triceratops was as intelligent as the T Rex
3 The Triceratops was as tall as the Stegosaurus
4 The Triceratops was not as dangerous as the T Rex

3
2 The book is not as funny as the film.
3 Mr Thomas is not as popular as Mr Brown.
4 English is not as difficult as Maths.
5 My present was not as expensive as your present.
6 Tennis is not as exciting as football.

Superlatives

1

adjective	comparative	superlative
old		the oldest
new	newer than	the newest
tall	taller than	the tallest
hot	hotter than	
big	bigger than	the biggest
pretty	prettier than	the prettiest
heavy		the heaviest
important	more important than	the most important
boring	more boring than	the most boring
relaxing	more relaxing than	
good	better than	the best
bad	worse than	the worst

2
2 the most difficult
3 worse than/more boring than
4 the prettiest
5 better than
6 the best
7 better than/more relaxing than
8 the worst

3

	Dick Spyder
money	
danger	
intelligence	

	Raymond Black
money	
danger	
intelligence	

	Edgar Peril
money	
danger	
intelligence	

	Lucy Diamond
money	
danger	
intelligence	

4
2 is more intelligent than
3 is not as dangerous as
4 is more intelligent than
5 is richer than
6 is not as intelligent as
7 is the most dangerous
8 is the richest

5
2 I'm the funniest person in the family.
3 I'm as pretty as my mum.
4 Our dog is older than me (by two weeks!).
5 My sister isn't as intelligent as me (but she thinks she is).
6 My youngest brother is older than me (it's possible – think about it).
7 He isn't as funny as my dad thinks he is.
8 My dad is the richest but he's also the meanest.

Directions (prepositions of place)

1
2 in front of
3 round the corner
4 opposite
5 on the corner
6 behind

2
2 Go round the corner.
3 Go straight ahead.
4 It's in front of the bank.
5 It's next to the supermarket.
6 Take the first right.
7 Take the second left.

3
2 post office
3 church
4 cinema
5 bank
6 hospital

4
1 Go straight ahead. Take the second right. It's opposite the chemist's, on the left.
2 Go straight ahead. Take the second right. It's at the end of the street, on the right, opposite the hospital.
3 Go straight ahead. Take the second left. Go to the end of the street, it's on the left, opposite the post office.
4 Go straight ahead. Take the third left. It's on the corner of high Street, on the left, opposite the church.
5 Go straight ahead. Take the second left. Go to the end of the street. It's on the corner of West Street, opposite the tourist office.
6 Go straight ahead. Take the fourth right. It's opposite the park, on the left.

have to / don't have to

1 a 4 b 5 c 1 d 3 e 6 f 2

2
2 You have to come to my party.
3 My brother doesn't have to study hard.
4 She has to write a story for homework.
5 We don't have to go to school tomorrow.
6 I have to tidy my room every weekend.
7 We don't have to do the washing-up.
8 Do you have to wear a uniform to school?

3 2 g 3 f 4 a 5 h 6 e 7 b 8 d

4
2 have to leave
3 don't have to switch
4 have to use
5 have to talk
6 don't have to take
7 have to wave
8 have to wiggle
9 don't have to work
10 don't have to be

5
3 has to study hard before a test.
4 doesn't have to leave home early to go to school.
5 doesn't have to wear a school uniform.
6 doesn't have to help with the housework.
7 has to study hard for the test.
8 has to leave home early to go to school.
9 have to wear a school uniform.
10 have to help with the housework.
11 don't have to study hard for the test.
12 don't have to leave home early to go to school.

going to – negative

1
2 going to cook
3 going to be
4 going to meet
5 going to give
6 going to ask
7 going to fight
8 going to have

2
1 It's
2 You're
3 is
4 isn't
5 are
6 aren't
7 You're
8 you aren't

might (not)

1
1 It might rain.
2 You might have an accident.
3 You might not have enough money.
4 You might get hungry.
5 Your teachers might not like it.
6 I might not have any more children.

2
2 might not
3 might
4 might not
5 might not
6 might
7 might
8 might

3 a 6 b 8 c 2 d 9 e 3 f 5 g 7 h 4 i 1

4
2 're going to
3 might – might
4 going to
5 are going to
6 might
7 not going to
8 're not going to

Past simple (regular and irregular)

1
2 opened
3 listened
4 talked
5 laughed
6 looked
7 asked
8 walked
9 took
10 went
11 saw
12 won
13 came
14 knew
15 sang
16 ran

2
1 took
2 had
3 broke
4 found
5 sang
6 caught
7 went
8 thought

3
2 arrived
3 danced
4 tried
5 studied
6 went
7 saw
8 climbed
9 took
10 brought
11 bought
12 sang
13 laughed
14 found
15 travelled
16 thought

4
2 went to London by train. He didn't go by plane.
3 met Sally. She didn't meet Anne.
4 played squash. They didn't play tennis.
5 had a bath. He didn't have a shower.
6 broke her arm. She didn't break her leg.
7 studied. He didn't meet his friends.
8 watched TV. We didn't go to the cinema.

5
1 thought
2 had
3 gave
4 hated
5 said
6 ↓ walked
6 → went
7 found
8 lost
9 saw
10 took
11 got
12 opened

6
2 watched
3 Did you like
4 wasn't
5 was
6 lost
7 went
8 took
9 did you go
10 had
11 thought
12 said
13 didn't want
14 told

7
2 didn't like
3 didn't take
4 didn't write
5 didn't go
6 didn't find
7 didn't ask
8 didn't hear

8
2 went
3 happened
4 found
5 did you do
6 Did you open
7 opened
8 was
9 Did you take
10 didn't take
11 took
12 Did
13 ask
14 got
15 phoned
16 came
17 got
18 Was
19 said
20 gave

Past time expressions

1
2 ago
3 later
4 After
5 One – next
6 Finally

2
2 One day
3 After thirty minutes
4 ten minutes later
5 Finally
6 The next day

some / any

1 1 g 2 f 3 b 4 a 5 d 6 h 7 c 8 e

2 1 d 2 e 3 a 4 h 5 g 6 b 7 c 8 f

3
2 I'd like some information about concerts.
3 Can I have some eggs and some cheese please?
4 Is there any yoghurt in the fridge?
5 Let's go out and have some fun.
6 I'm going to buy some medicine for my cold.

4
2 any money
3 any kids
4 some examples
5 some kids
6 some money

5
2 There aren't any bicycles.
3 There aren't any kids.
4 There are some dogs.
5 There aren't any cats.
6 There are some shops.

6
2 **A**: some, **B**: any
3 **A**: some, **B**: any
4 **A**: any, **B**: some
5 **A**: some, **B**: some

Irregular plurals

1
2 foot
3 women
4 tooth
5 goose
6 child
7 teeth
8 children
9 feet
10 people
11 person
12 woman

2
2 knives
3 thieves
4 leaves
5 fish
6 sheep

3
2 leaves
3 foot
4 goose
5 tooth
6 knife
7 children
8 thieves

Questions with *who*

1
1 e 2 c 3 a
4 f 5 d 6 b

2
2 sent you a/the valentine card
3 paid for your new computer
4 wants to watch another DVD
5 called the police

3
1 Who plays the new Batman?
2 Who sings this song?
3 Who wants to eat now?
4 Who gave you that lovely jumper?
5 Who phoned you last night?

4
1 4 2 2 3 5 4 3 5 1

like (doing)

1
2 singing
3 reading
4 climbing
5 watching
6 dancing
7 going
8 taking

2
2 loves swimming. She likes talking on the phone but she doesn't like shopping. She hates reading.
3 love talking on the phone. They like shopping but they don't like reading. They hate swimming.

must / mustn't

1
2 f 3 e 4 b 5 c 6 a

2
2 must wake up
3 mustn't hang
4 mustn't ride your bicycle
5 must switch lights
6 mustn't bring animals into

3
2 mustn't be
3 must wear
4 mustn't put
5 mustn't eat
6 mustn't touch
7 mustn't jump
8 mustn't climb

Adverbs of manner

1 **2**

adjective	adverb
angry	angrily
bright	brightly
careful	carefully
clever	cleverly
dangerous	dangerously
easy	easily
fast	fast
furious	furiously
nervous	nervously

3
bad – badly
clever – cleverly
boring – boringly
happy – happily
tired – tiredly
good – well
fast – fast
serious – seriously
excited – excitedly
easy – easily
terrible – terribly

4
slowly – quickly
brilliantly – terribly
loudly – quietly
badly – well
happily – sadly

5
1 badly
2 furiously
3 easily
4 brightly
6 brilliantly
7 fast
8 carefully

6
2 adjective
3 adjective
4 adverb
5 adverb
6 adjective
7 adjective
8 adverb

7
2 loudly
3 quietly
4 happily
5 angrily
6 carefully
7 dangerously
8 furiously

8
2 quickly
3 quietly
4 loudly
5 excitedly
6 seriously
7 nervously
8 intelligently

9
1 rich
2 sharp
3 carefully
4 quickly
5 excitedly
6 quietly
7 excited
8 bright
9 quickly
10 seriously

10
2 badly
3 slowly
4 rudely
5 angrily
6 furiously
7 intelligently
8 loudly
9 nervously
10 well

12
2 It was an easy Maths test and I finished quickly.
3 I walked slowly because I had a heavy bag.
4 It was a lovely summer day and the sun shone brightly.
5 I had to talk loudly because it was a noisy party.
6 The children got up early and opened their presents excitedly.
7 My dad drove dangerously and we were all nervous passengers.
8 It was a brilliant song and she sang it well.

whose + possessive *'s*

1
2 It's Batman's car.
3 It's Mickey Mouse's ear.
4 It's Superman's cape.
5 It's Spiderman's mask.
6 It's Sherlock Holmes' pipe.
7 It's Harry Potter's wand.
8 It's Marge Simpson's hair.

2
2 **A** Whose is this watch?
B It's Amanda's.
3 **A** Whose are these boots?
B They're Lois'.
4 **A** Whose is this belt?
B It's Lois'.
5 **A** Whose is this hat?
B It's Amanda's.
6 **A** Whose are these glasses?
B They're Amanda's.
7 **A** Whose is this mobile/phone/mobile phone?
B It's Kerry's.
8 **A** Whose is this handbag?
B It's Lois'.

Possessive pronouns

1
my – mine
your – yours
his – his
her – hers
our – ours
their – theirs

2
2 hers 3 ours 4 theirs
5 our 6 Their 7 yours
8 her

3
1 The laptop is theirs.
2 The rabbit is ours.
3 The MP3-player is hers.
4 The backpack is his.
5 The football is mine.

4
2 mine 3 mine 4 ours
5 his 6 his

5
2 my
3 his
4 your
5 mine
6 her
7 yours
8 their
9 theirs
10 yours
11 ours
12 Whose
13 your
14 my
15 your
16 mine

Past participles

1 2 seen 3 come 4 cut 5 been 6 taken 7 won 8 broken 9 bought 10 fallen 11 lost 12 had

3 2 had 3 gone 4 bought 5 won 6 cut 7 taken 8 lost

Present perfect

1
2 It hasn't rained for a long time.
3 I've bought a new book.
4 My parents haven't seen this film.
5 He's always worked here.
6 We haven't eaten our lunch.
7 You've listened to all my CDs.
8 My favourite band's made a new CD.

2 2 g 3 a 4 f 5 e 6 h 7 b

3
2 We haven't moved house.
3 They haven't come back from their holiday.
4 I haven't studied for tomorrow's test.
5 My dad hasn't made dinner.

4 2 g 3 k 4 a 5 b 6 i 7 l 8 c 9 d 10 h 11 j 12 f

5
2 have – done
3 've / have tidied
4 've / have done
5 Have – fed
6 've / have cleaned
7 've / have been
8 Have – cooked

6
2 Timothy hasn't phoned me.
3 I've been windsurfing three times.
4 I've travelled to lots of different countries.
5 I've read this book four times.
6 Tess has eaten all the chocolate.
7 Have you heard their new CD?
8 Has the teacher given us any homework?

7 2 climbed 3 swum 4 walked 5 taken 6 made 7 learned 8 written 9 found

8
2 haven't / have not listened
3 've / have eaten
4 haven't / have not opened
5 've / have seen
6 's / has travelled
7 's / has won
8 haven't / have not learned
9 's / has worked
10 hasn't / has not written

9
2 've / have been
3 's / has won
4 's / has beaten
5 have – been
6 's / has tried
7 's / has been
8 's / has visited
9 's / has enjoyed
10 hasn't / has not invited

Present perfect + *already / yet*

1 1 d 2 e 3 f 4 c 5 b 6 g 7 a 8 h

2
2 already broken
3 18 yet
4 already competed
5 US yet
6 already earned
7 already attracted
8 gold medal yet

3
2 She hasn't spoken to me yet.
3 Henry's already written the email.
4 I've already asked my mum.
5 My dad's already found a new job.
6 They haven't invited me to their party yet.
7 You've already told me that.
8 We haven't finished our lunch yet.

4
2 hasn't learned – 's / has – got
3 's / has – done – haven't finished
4 haven't asked – 've / have – given
5 haven't seen – 's / has – told
6 've / have – taken – hasn't stopped
7 's / has – turned – hasn't got
8 hasn't used – 's / has – broken

5 2 already 3 yet 4 already 5 already 6 already

6
2 Have you played Kingdom of Doom? – g
3 Have you sold your computer? – f
4 Have you fixed your bike? – b
5 Has she invited you to her party? – h
6 Has she given you a birthday present? – c
7 Has he done the washing up? – a
8 Has he finished the book? – d

7
2 He hasn't done the washing-up yet.
3 He's already tidied the living room.
4 He's already walked the dog.
5 He hasn't gone shopping yet.
6 He hasn't cooked breakfast yet.
7 He's already put the rubbish out.
8 He hasn't paid the telephone bill yet.

8 2 False 3 False 4 False 5 True 6 True 7 False 8 True

9
2 He's already told me your secret.
3 We haven't had lunch yet.
4 Paula's just gone to the shops.
5 The dog's already had its puppies.
6 Don hasn't bought a new car yet.
7 Mum's just broken a cup.
8 I haven't sent him the email yet.

10
2 've / have already had
3 've / have already been
4 've / have already seen
5 haven't met – yet
6 haven't seen – yet
7 's / has already promised
8 haven't done – yet
9 haven't bought – yet
10 haven't travelled – yet
11 've / have already got

11
2 We've just bought a new TV.
3 She hasn't woken up yet.
4 You've already had two sandwiches.
5 They've just finished playing computer games.
6 My mum's just had a new baby.
7 I haven't seen the new Batman film yet.
8 I've already taken the dog for a walk.

12
2 Oliver hasn't given me a present yet.
3 She's already phoned her mum.
4 Mum and dad haven't gone out yet.
5 I haven't done my exams yet.
6 They've already had dinner.
7 Sally hasn't sold her skateboard yet.
8 We've already found our dog.

So (do/have) I / Neither (do/have) I

1
2 So do I
3 So have I
4 So have I
5 Neither do I
6 Neither do I
7 Neither have I
8 Neither have I

2
2 So do I.
3 So have I.
4 Neither do I.
5 Neither have I.
6 Neither do I.
7 So have I.
8 So do I.

3 2 h 3 a 4 f 5 b 6 c 7 d 8 g

4
2 So have I.
3 neither have I.
4 So do I.
5 Neither do I.
6 So do I.
7 So have I.
8 Neither have I.
9 so do I.

5
2 So
3 So
4 Neither
5 Neither
6 Neither
7 Neither
8 So

6
2 Neither did I.
3 Neither can I.
4 Neither do I.
5 So did I.
6 So do I.
7 So have I.
8 So can I.

Present perfect + *ever / never*

1
1 eaten
2 ever
3 Paris
4 Have
5 foreign
6 never
7 holidays
8 stay
9 found
10 phone
11 done
12 please

2
1 b 2 g 3 e 4 a
5 f 6 h 7 c 8 d

3
1 Have you ever had a dog?
2 She's never had an accident.
3 They've never been on an airplane.
4 Has she ever met a famous person?
5 We've never been to a fancy dress party.

4
1 've had
2 've fallen into
3 've fallen out
4 've fallen off
5 've crashed
6 have you ever broken
7 've broken
8 haven't broken
9 've never broken
10 've been on TV
11 've met some famous people
12 've written
13 have you ever thought
14 've never thought

5
2 Have you ever fallen asleep in class?
3 Have you ever been on TV?
4 Have you ever won a competition?/ Have you ever won the first prize in a competition?
5 Have you ever eaten with chopsticks?
6 Have you ever been in/to Paris?
7 Have you ever travelled by helicopter?
8 Have you ever driven a car?

will-future

1
2 I won't be late.
3 There won't be any fog.
4 My father'll come and pick us up.
5 The rain'll stop soon.
6 I won't come to your house tomorrow.

2
2 'll rain
3 'll be
4 'll go
5 won't bite
6 'll like
7 won't be
8 won't sleep

3
a 2 b 7 d 8 e 6
f 5 g 4 h 3

4
2 she'll call / phone
3 he'll wash the car
4 she won't go shopping
5 he won't play football
6 I'll study English

5
2 won't know
3 won't be
4 'll phone
5 'll have
6 'll invite
7 won't come
8 'll stay
9 won't kill

6
2 'll be
3 'll live
4 'll get
5 'll have
6 'll take
7 'll send
8 won't have